157 Questions to Ask When Looking For the Right Horse Boarding Stable

By
Sheri Grunska

The horse owner's guide to finding the best stable for you and your horse

Edited
by
Martha Schultz

Cover picture by
Shutterstock images

Acknowledgments

I want to thank my husband David for all his support and love. He is my rock when life gets bumpy. I wanted to give a special thank you to Martha Schultz, who listens to my ideas and offers encouragement and honest direction when I am writing. I have always had this passion to write books and it has always been important for me to have a certain depth with each book I write so that I can educate my readers and open their eyes to new things regarding horse care. Martha has been a champion when encouraging me to write subjects that are "outside the box" which at times can be intimidating for an author. For that I am forever grateful.

I also want to thank the people who shared their stories in this book in order to help others. The more we talk about the realities of horse care both good and sometimes not so good, the more we will change the industry for the betterment of the horse.

Table of Contents

Make the proper daily care of your horse a priority and your horse will thank you in many ways.

The Reason I Wrote This Book

You LOVE your horse and you want the best for him and the weight of that responsibility falls on you as you learn what he needs to thrive and feel safe in his surroundings. This book is very educational, useful and I also believe vital for the horse owner who needs to board their horse. New horse owners will especially benefit because it will help you develop the knowledge and tools to make well-informed decisions when choosing a boarding stable for your horse. This is a subject that has not been written about before in a "question and answer" format yet it is so important for the health and well-being of your horse and for you as the horse owner.

I felt it was very important to write this book because I have witnessed first-hand what can happen when a horse owner chooses a boarding stable that turns out to be a poor decision. This same scenario has probably happened at least one time to almost every person who has ever boarded their horse – including me! Now as the owner of a large boarding facility for fifteen years, I have heard many stories about boarding stables that turned out not to be a good fit and for many different reasons. Sometimes the problem was not at all about the care of the horses. It could have been an issue with any range of things such as the social atmosphere or poor barn management. It could be that your horse has aged and needs a quieter setting for his senior years, especially as his special needs have increased. It could also be that you have grown in your horsemanship and want to improve your riding skills and start competing. The reasons why a person selects or changes boarding stables are endless, but I wanted to provide insights into the world of horse boarding in order to prepare you for the unexpected and assist you in making well informed decisions.

Many horse owners put a lot of value on the horse trainer and the saddle and tack they purchase for their horse BUT they neglect one of the most important elements of all – the boarding stable! You need to remember that the trainer will only be working with your horse periodically but the daily care is continuous! You can have a wonderful trainer and the most expensive saddle but if your horse is stressed out due to the living conditions then you are going to have issues. If your horse is not able to feel safe in his surroundings or have enough food, fresh water or proper shelter then you are going to have a horse who may become anxious or develop anxiety and then nothing else matters until you resolve your horses primary needs.

I have watched many horse owners choose a stable without knowing what questions to ask to make sure they choose a place that will fit their needs and, more importantly, their horse's needs. Without a sound decision making process while selecting a stable, frustration and regret will often follow. This book is written to provide the horse owner with the knowledge and tools to make educated decisions about the care of their horse and selection of an appropriate boarding stable for their horse.

What is the most important thing you want in a boarding stable? Your answers may change after you read this book! When looking for a boarding stable and touring facilities you should have a discussion with the barn managers about what they offer and what you want in a stable. In order to do this, you need to know what to ask. This book will help provide the framework for evaluating stables and save you stress and heartache down the road. By aligning your expectations with the stable management and protocols you will be prepared to ask relevant questions, understand management decisions, and compromise when appropriate in order to maintain and strengthen your barn relationships.

I love to tour boarding stables and, after doing consulting with many barns and helping them develop the boarding business they want to have, I have learned that to have a sustainable relationship between the barn owner and the horse owner, they both need to have a realistic understanding of what they want. For the barn owner it's about knowing what kind of boarding stable they want to operate and what services they can provide and for the horse owner it is about knowing if a stable can meet their needs. The goal of this book is to help you find the right boarding stable the first time NOT after several moves and adjustments for both the horse owner and the horse.

You are going to get to know your horse in ways you never imagined and by the end of this book you will be well on your way to understanding what your horse needs for proper care and how each boarding stable can or cannot meet his needs.

This may be one of the most consequential books you read when it comes to your horse's health and well-being. If you get those two things right the rest will start to fall in place so you can focus on developing your relationship with your horse and development of your horsemanship and riding skills. Don't underestimate the importance of finding the right boarding stable for you and where the care is top-notch for your horse.

Chapter 1

Let's Talk About Your Horse

You have just made all your dreams come true. You have found your dream horse and you are in heaven! You have made a promise that you are going to do everything possible to make sure the love of your life – your horse, is going to stay healthy, safe and happy. So, where do you begin?

If you are a new horse owner then this process of looking for a boarding stable can seem daunting, especially if you are new to the world of boarding horses. You may have driven by a few horse stables and you are impressed by how they look on the outside. You can look on Facebook or even google horse boarding stables in your area and find websites for boarding businesses near you and they all look fantastic online. This is where educating yourself as a horse owner will be one of the most important things you can do to ensure that you find the best place with proper care for your horse and you. Educating yourself and knowing what questions to ask will help ensure that the stable you choose is a good fit for your needs at the time. Get ready to learn a lot because by the time you finish this book you are going to be skilled on what questions to ask to make sure your horse will be cared for in the manner you envisioned.

The best place to start (and a very important part!) is to learn everything you can about your horse so that you know what questions to ask when looking for a boarding stable. Let's start at the very beginning.

1. What breed of horse do you own?

There are many different types of boarding stables and training barns and some are breed and discipline specific. For example – If you are looking at a breed specific type of training barn and you own a Quarter horse, then it would seem appropriate to either board your horse at a stable that accepts all breeds of horses or a barn that is mainly a show barn where most of its clients go to the Quarter horse shows to compete. The same would be true for the reining horse, ranch horse discipline or any other specific breed or riding disciplines. **It doesn't mean this is the rule**, but if you have a Saddlebred and are riding saddle seat then you will probably have a hard time fitting in at a barn where everyone else is riding western pleasure or doing halter competition. You also might have a difficult time finding the right trainer at this type of barn for your Saddlebred. Most multi-discipline boarding stables have accommodations for all breeds of horses.

The breed of horse you own could influence what type of boarding you are looking for. If you live in the Midwest where the temperatures can plummet below zero then you might want to rethink outdoor "rough" board (where the horse lives outside 24/7) for a hard-keeper, thin skinned horse like a Thoroughbred. They don't grow much of a winter coat, are vulnerable and can become cold easily in harsh temperatures. There are exceptions to the rule, but for the horse that doesn't grow a thick coat - having a stall each evening for them to eat and rest is beneficial. Now if you own a draft type horse that grows a heavy winter coat, he will do better being outside 24/7. Most horses do great outside if they have shelter from the wind and rain and plenty of good quality hay and water to drink especially as the temperatures drop. Again, it will depend on the breed of horse and a few other important factors that we will discuss in this book.

2. What age is your horse? A very young horse or an older senior horse can make a huge difference when looking for a stable.

10 years

When looking for a boarding stable you will want to make sure they can accommodate your horse if he is either very young (under a year old) or is a much older senior horse that now has slowed down and will do better in a smaller herd setting. Both types of horses have their own special needs as they age and can require a little more care from the stable. We will talk more in a later chapter about age and the proper care of your horse.

3. Is your horse nervous or calm?

calm

You're going to want to learn everything about your horse and his personality. Is he nervous or become agitated easily? Is he very easy going in new environments? This will be important when moving him to his new home and getting him settled into his new surroundings with new pasture buddies and herd structure.

4. Is your horse used to being in a herd turnout, private turnout or has he been stalled most of his life with little or no turnout?

It will benefit you to know the boarding history of your horse. I know this is not always possible, but it helps the barn owner/manager in placing him in a suitable herd. If he has been in a herd of horses previously, then he will understand the herd dynamics and probably be "street smart" when it comes to figuring out his place in his new herd. His age can play a part in this also since very young horses will experience new things every day and they will be learning a lot through their interactions with pasture mates.

Another scenario that can present itself happens with the horse that has never been with other horses in a herd setting. Often horses that are "show horses"

16

Stalled - night

will be stalled for many hours or in private turnout so they don't get the full experience of herd life and behavior. The hardest and most challenging horses I have had to place in a herd were always show horses who have never lived with other horses in a herd of any size, and now for the first time, they are allowed to be a horse and all that comes with it. It can be a huge transition for some horses, especially if they are insecure or timid. It has taken me as long as a month in one rare situation to get a new horse to finally find a buddy and settle in. Once he found a friend and understood life in a herd, he flourished!

Some horses do great on private turnout while others pace the fence and you can easily see they are stressed or agitated because they are separated from the other horses. Your horse's response to a new setting will completely depend on his personality and history so he will need to be watched closely, especially if private turnout is something new for him.

5. What is your horse's position in the herd? Is your horse dominant with other horses or at the bottom of the pecking order?

2nd command

After many years of boarding horses for a business I have learned that many people do not know if their horse is dominant or not. As a new horse owner you may not know this answer, and that is perfectly understandable. If the barn manager is knowledgeable and experienced in horse behavior and herd management they should be able to figure it out quickly. Knowing if a horse is dominant or not can make a difference in determining the herd in which they are going to be most compatible. The goal is to have the least amount of kicking, biting and aggressive behavior from all horses and if the barn manager knows the horses at the stable well, then it makes the job much easier.

I will always ask a person who is on a tour at my stable about the personality of their horse. Are they dominant or are they very timid? Any information I can get will always help me put together a plan of action. The last thing I want is a horse getting hurt or injured and that should be the goal of every stable.

6. Will your horse be blanketed during the winter months or not?

When thinking about the horse you own, you will want to decide if he will need to be blanketed during the colder winter months. Of course, this will also depend on the horse and type of winter weather you have in your area. The reason I want you to start thinking about blanketing is because you will want to find out if the stable will blanket your horse as a service. You will also want to know what they charge if you are not able to do the blanketing. This will include fly sheets, turnout sheets and winter blankets. We will get into this in much more detail in a later chapter. *Fly mask/Fly spray*

7. Does your horse have any vices that you will need to share with the barn manager?

We would all love to think our horse is perfect but they each have their own quirks and vices. If you have owned your horse for a long time, then you probably know his quirks and vices. If you are a new horse owner, then it is important to learn what vices your horse may have. If you are not aware of any, then the barn manager should let you know if any develop so together you both can create a positive plan of action to manage and minimize them as much as possible. Some vices are hard to stop but occasionally you can change things around in the horse's environment and the vice will disappear. Often the reasons for the vice could be stress or previous circumstances that have created bad habits that are hard to break.

Vices can show themselves in many different forms. Biting and kicking are two that people commonly think of but even a nip here and there can become annoying and HURT! Horses can pick up habits such as pulling away when leading them, to the point where you need to use a chain to curb the behavior. You might have a horse that has food aggression that developed from a previous bad experience and this can make things dangerous when cleaning a stall with this type of horse in the stall at the same time. Cribbing (crib-biting and windsucking)

likes stall mates that are docile, not agressive/a

18

Clean H2O
Likas clean heavy on bedding stall
does not chew on stall/door etc

is a vice that not only is unhealthy for the horse, but it destroys things also. Some horses that have been stalled for a very long time will begin weaving back and forth as way of dealing with the boredom or stress they are feeling.

The most important thing about vices is that you want to make sure the people who are working and handling the horses are safe. When a horse has a vice that has been identified, then it becomes much easier to create an effective plan of action that is both positive for the horse and safe for the employees.

Suppliments

8. Does your horse have special needs that will require dietary or medical attention daily?

It is important to learn if your horse has any special needs - which many of them do! It can, and most likely will, make a difference when choosing a boarding stable. For example, if your horse has special dietary needs or physical needs then that should to be taken into consideration when selecting a stable. The same will be true for the horse with vision problems or neurological issues. The very young horse and of course the older senior horse may have special needs as they age. Many stables are not able to accommodate the horse with special needs so the more you can learn about the boarding stable and what they are able to provide for your horse, the better your decision making will be.

Easy Keeper - supplements - hay high quality

9. Is your horse a *hard keeper* or *easy keeper* regarding his weight?

Some horses look at hay and gain weight (not really but it sure seems like it!) and others can eat all day long and never gain a pound. What type of horse do you own? Is he an easy keeper (keeps weight on easily) or does he need extra hay and grain to keep weight on? Is he being exercised a lot and consequently needs the extra calories? Is he young and growing and needs extra food daily? Has he become old and now doesn't eat his hay as well as he used to, so you need to supplement it with a high calorie senior grain? These things are important to

Special needs:
Graze: gut-fill from awake
to sleep

know when looking for a stable so that you can ask the right questions to see if the stable can accommodate your horse's special needs.

The same is very true for the overweight horse that needs a grazing muzzle when the horses are on pasture during the summertime. What if your horse is overweight to the point of developing laminitis and he is living outside in a herd with unlimited hay available 24-hours a day? This will pose a great health risk for the horse! These are important things to know about your horse and to consider when you start looking for a boarding stable.

want a calm quite barn/not teenagers

10. Will your horse be ridden by a young person or an adult?

adult grandchild

When you start thinking about boarding stables, finding a good fit will also include the person who will be coming to the barn often and riding. Some barns have many young people and the atmosphere is very busy and even crazy at times! This can be fun but it may not be for everyone. Many older people or timid and insecure riders prefer a quiet barn that doesn't have much activity. They feel more comfortable riding when the arena is empty. Some people get very nervous if there are too many horses in the arena while others thrive on it. At the end of the day, you need to find a barn that best suits you, especially if you are an inexperienced or timid rider.

11. Will your horse be ridden by a novice rider or an experienced rider?

growth in riding
Western trainer
Some one who educates the owners about horses.

The experience of the person handling and riding a horse will greatly factor into what type of barn is a good fit. The best type of a barn is the one that offers encouragement and education to the new horse owner without judgement. Of course, every barn would love to say they nurture inexperienced riders, but the truth is some barns are set up for the more experienced riders with higher level riding and instructors. Finding a good fit is important for personal growth in your horsemanship.

20

12. Is your horse completely "finished" (trained) or will you be looking for a riding instructor/trainer? — Clicker, Rt, trail safety / First Aid

This is very important! If you are an experienced rider and your horse is finished, you may not need an instructor except for a tune-up here or there. Often these types of riders love to do clinics on the side to help them refine certain skills and because they simply love to learn and grow in their skills and horsemanship. We have riders at our barn who are very experienced but continue their education in riding so that they grow and learn new things. They want to be current on the latest trends and improve their relationship with their horse.

If you will need a trainer for your horse or an instructor for you, then it will be important to make sure the stable you are looking at offers on-site trainers or provides the option of bringing in a trainer of your chosen discipline or skill level.

13. Will you be showing or just casual riding? / trail

Most boarding stables are, for the most part, multi-discipline barns that will welcome all kinds of horses and riders. Some stables will tend to gravitate towards certain types of riding disciplines and activities. If you are someone who doesn't ride but comes out to the barn just to hang out with your horse then a barn where every person shows horses and every horse is in full time training might not be a perfect fit for you. The same would be true for the person who heavily competes on the show circuit - You might prefer to be at a stable where you can make friends with other people who compete and have common goals.

14. What choice of riding discipline do you plan on doing?

It is not a necessity that you decide what type of riding discipline you want to do in order to find the right boarding stable, but it can make things nicer for you to be at a stable where other's riding interests are similar. It is a great way to connect and learn together in the riding discipline of your choice. You might even change disciplines down the road (which happens a lot) as your skills and interests advance. You will then need to decide if your current barn is still a good fit or if it is time to look for a different stable to better accommodate your new interests.

Ask the barn manager what types of riders are at the barn. A multi-discipline barn can be advantageous because you will see so many different styles of riding and breeds of horses. You might even decide to switch riding disciplines as you become a more confident rider and focus on a primary discipline or interest. I have seen many people start off riding one discipline and change as they watch others doing something that looks interesting. Variety is the spice of life!

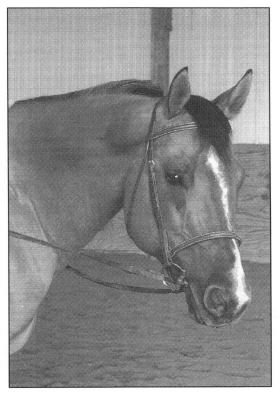

I chose the first boarding stable I toured because I was a new horse owner and I really didn't know what I should be looking for in a stable. I was sold even before I toured the stable because the place had a beautiful website and I was in love with the dream.

The place was beautiful but I didn't realize _how busy the facility was_ and I found myself not wanting to go out to the barn after a month or two because there were always two or three horses in the arena. I was shy and insecure about my riding so I missed out on several months of growing in my horsemanship because I would only get my horse out and brush him then leave quickly.

For that period of time in my life, that particular barn was not a good fit for me even though the care was excellent. I ended up leaving after about six months to find a better fit for me at that time. The first stable choice was a wonderful facility and had great care but I was not growing and I really needed a place where I could try new things and not feel intimidated.

If I needed to move my horse today, I would gladly go back to that first boarding stable. I am much more confident when riding with others in the arena and now I actually enjoy it!

Cathy

Chapter 2

Boarding Stables and What They Offer

Looking for a boarding stable for your horse can be both exciting and overwhelming, especially if you are a new horse owner and you don't know what to look for in services and care for your horse. The chapters ahead are going to lay out an easy and orderly set of questions that will help shape what you want for you and your horse. They may also bring to light many things you would have never thought of when it comes to boarding stables and the difference in care and amenities that they offer.

When reviewing stables online it is important that you don't get caught up in how nice the images look or how well written the description of amenities is. I want to educate you and give you the knowledge so that you can use good judgement and be discriminating when choosing a boarding stable. Every barn owner and manager will do things a little differently and that doesn't necessarily mean that one place is better than another. But the reality is that some stables provide a higher level of understanding, experience and attentiveness while caring for the health and well-being of the horses and they employ sound principles of care that focus on the physical and mental well-being of your horse. It also means you will be happier if you find a stable that has the same ideas and care practices that you embrace, and your horse requires.

When you drive up to a stable that is gorgeous on the outside it is important that you learn to dig deeper to make sure it is the right fit for your horse and you. You need to remember that just because a stable seems perfect on the outside doesn't mean that it is on the inside. Sorry to burst your bubble! Be smart and take your time and really get to know what you are looking for as a possible barn home for your horse and you.

It will help you understand different barn practices if you appreciate the fact that you are dealing with a **business relationship**. Horse boarding stables are businesses just like any other business except for one major difference, they are taking care of a very large animal and with that comes a different kind of responsibility. For most barn owners and barn managers this is a true passion and they get into the business because they love horses. It is also a 24/7 day job, every day of the year and many barn owners and managers live right on the property which makes this career very unique.

Boarding stables will change and evolve as the owners of the business decide what type of barn they want to have. They might start out as a barn that caters to kids that show horses but years down the road they may change and become more of a barn where the clients do a lot of trail riding. It doesn't happen at every stable but is does happen and this could mean changes for you as a client. Finding a stable that is a great fit takes time and effort and requires that you learn about what each stable offers to meet your needs.

I have listed many questions in the pages ahead that will help guide your decision process.

15. How long has the stable been in business?

This question is not a deal breaker, but I do want to make you aware of a couple things in regards to brand new business ownership. Truth – if you are going to board your horse at a new stable then understand that along with every other new business ever started, there will be many changes during the first year or two. It is only natural for a new business owner to make changes as they start to experience what the finances and workload looks like year-round.

Most new stable owners do not go into owning a boarding business with the intention of making changes, but it happens and it is a natural consequence of experience and improvement. Our boarding stable was no exception. I made many changes during the first couple of years because I didn't fully realize all the work it was going to be, or all the costs involved to keep the barn up and running.

It was much more challenging than I expected and planned for, hence many changes were required during our first two to three years in business.

It doesn't mean a brand-new boarding stable is a bad place to board a horse. It just means that you might see some changes that will affect you and your horse. While change is almost always disruptive, remember that not all changes are bad. The changes the barn owner is making might be wonderful improvements for the care of your horse and the atmosphere of the barn.

The Differences Between a Training Barn and a Boarding Stable

16. Is this a training barn or general boarding stable?

A training barn and boarding stable can have some differences that are important considerations. Often a "training barn" will have a head trainer where they have horses coming in for training for a set amount of time depending on what the owner wants and the horse needs. A training barn can have boarders but usually the main focus is training horses or horse/rider combo and you could be asked to take a certain number of lessons each week in order to stay at that specific barn. The biggest thing to think about is that you might have a lot more activity with horses coming and going depending on the training program. Often you will hear that a horse is in for 30, 60 or 90 days of training or a tune-up and then the horse leaves. That means that there will be a lot of movement in the herd composition and herd restructuring will be the norm.

Training barns can be a good fit for someone who has a young horse that needs to be trained several days a week. It can also be ideal for the person who has a horse in training and who participates in showing with the support of the trainer attending the shows with them. There are pros and cons to both types of boarding stables as you will learn as you continue reading. Often a website will give clues about the type of stable they are and once you make your initial call you will be able to find out in more detail what their main focus is.

A general boarding barn can have many different breeds, riding disciplines and trainers at the stable, depending on the size. This type of barn may be more relaxed in that you aren't under the instruction of the trainer and subject to their requirements for your horse when you come out to casually ride. Most general boarding stables tend to be more casual and often many of the riders will not be in a structured lesson program.

17. Is the barn heated during the winter?

If you live in an area that gets extremely cold, then you will find barns that are temperature controlled and heated. This is always wonderful for the horse owner but does present many other things to think about for your horse. Blanketing will become much more important if the temperatures fluctuate so much that you need to change blankets when the horse goes outside for the day and then again when he comes in. The last thing you want is a sick horse so you will want to make sure that the staff is knowledgeable when it comes to changing blankets and can determine what type of blanket to put on your horse so he doesn't become overheated in the barn after being outside all day in much colder temps.

If you are considering a heated barn, then you will want to pay close attention to the ventilation in the stable area. It is important that the stable has efficient air flow and the air doesn't smell of urine (ammonia smell). Horses can get respiratory issues quickly if they are confined in an enclosed area with poor ventilation and air circulation.

If you are looking at a barn that is not heated, then you will have much less to worry about and fewer blanket changes because the barn itself will be cold and the difference from being inside to outside will not be significant for blanketing.

18. Do you have a <u>bathroom & lounge on site?</u>

A <u>bathroom</u> is not a deal breaker for some people but it is an asset especially if you have a busy barn and many people are there for extended periods of time. Some stables don't have an indoor bathroom but will provide a Port-O-Potty.

Often a boarding stable will have a lounge where you can warm up on cold days or visit with other people. They may come with a kitchen or other amenities for you to use. The lounge may also offer windows for viewing the arena activity.

19. <u>Is there a wash stall with hot and cold water to bathe my horse?</u> washstall/hot/cold

If you live in an area that has warm or hot weather most of the year then you probably won't need hot water to hose off your horse. But if you live in a colder climate, then having a wash stall with hot and cold water is nice! Just something to think about especially when your horse is covered in mud! The wash stalls are often available seasonally in cold weather regions as the water lines are vulnerable to freezing and breakage.

The Horse Stalls

20. What size are the stalls?

Horse stalls come in many different sizes but the standard sizes are 12 x 12 or 10 x 12. Some barns will have some larger stalls to accommodate large horses or stalls for foaling if they accommodate birthing.

When it comes to your horse and the stall he will be living in, it is important to look at a few things regarding the stall itself. First – size is important especially if turnout

you have a larger horse. A 10 x 10 or 10 x 12 stall will be too small for many horses, especially the larger horses. Putting a large 16+ hand horse in a 10 x 10 stall will be tight and doesn't give him much room to move around or lay down. This can be hard on the horse if they are confined to their stalls for very long periods of time. 12 x 12 size stalls are a nice size and can accommodate most horses-even the large ones. Of course, adequate turnout is always important even if the stall is on the larger size so the horse can move and get exercise.

It is also important to note if the stall walls are solid between stalls or have grills so the horses can see each other. Horses are herd animals and they often feel more comfortable when they can see other horses next to them. Having solid walls isn't necessarily a bad thing but if your horse is an insecure horse or very nervous then having a horse next to him that he can see will often help alleviate stress.

Another point to bring up is the ventilation in the stable. If the stall walls are solid all the way up on each side of the stall then the air flow may be impaired and this can be hard on horses, especially if they are in a barn that is tightly closed up during the winter months. If this type of barn is heated, then it can make things a little stuffier with solid walls between each stall. It is always important to ask about the ventilation. Ventilation is very important and it will make a huge difference in how the barn feels and smells as well as the health of the horses.

If you are thinking of taking a stall, then ask to look at it and make sure it is in good condition. Look at the stall to see if it is free of sharp objects, nails or other hazards. If you find something in the stall that is sharp or broken, ask to have it fixed before you bring your horse to board there. Even a broken stall board can cause injury if a horse happens to kick out in his stall. It is amazing how horses can seem to find the one protruding nail in a horse stall and cut themselves on it.

21. What is the footing like for each stall – Rubber mats, gravel, cement etc?

The footing in each stall is important. You want the stall to have good drainage and not have large sink holes where the horse tends to stand. The footing for the stall is one of the most important things to look at because horses are big and heavy and you don't want stress on their legs from being on cement constantly. A barn that is designed well will have a good base in the stalls. An added plus are rubber mats to help keep the stall clean and reduce stress on the horse's legs. BEWARE – if your horse has to stand on cement with only a small amount of shavings then you are probably going to have issues down the road. The simple truth is that it is very hard on their legs. They are no different than us when we stand on cement for long periods of time. If the stall floor is dirt alone then ask the barn manager about drainage to make sure your horse isn't standing in a puddle of YUK constantly.

22. How much bedding do you provide each day?

Every boarding stable will handle bedding differently. Bedding will be one of the highest expenses for a boarding stable and there are many different opinions on types of bedding and how much to use. A lot will also depend on your horse and if he has any physical issues. If the footing is done right in a horse stall then you probably won't need a lot of bedding and your horse will do just fine. Ask to look at the stalls and how they are bedded and then you will have to decide if that is good for you and what you want for your horse.

23. How often do the stalls get cleaned daily – 1 or 2 times? How many days a week do they get cleaned?

Most boarding stables will clean the stalls one time a day as part of the daily care. Some facilities will clean the stalls twice a day and that is wonderful, but you need to realize that the service of "twice a day cleaning" comes with a price tag that will reflect the labor and extra shavings used. These types of barns tend to be upper-end and if you can afford it then that service is nice to have, especially if the horses are in due to inclement weather or an injury. Often a boarding stable will not clean on Sundays but will allow the owner of the horse to clean their stall if they choose. This is something you will want to discuss with the barn manager.

24. Can I clean my horse's stall and add extra shavings during the week if they are in due to inclement weather?

Often a client will want to pick their horse's stall if the horse is in during the day due to inclement weather. This is also true for the sick or injured horse. You will want to ask if this is allowed and if you can have additional shavings after you clean it. In most cases a barn will not allow someone to grab more shavings in these situations unless you have an arrangement and often there will be an extra fee for the cost of the bedding.

You will want to figure out what amount of bedding you feel comfortable with. If you do not like the way a particular stable beds their horses, do not be upset if they are not willing to change their policy for you. Boarding stables are a business and they need to keep things organized, especially if they have many horses to care for. They can't change things for every request but often they will try to be accommodating if it works for them as well. If the stall has great footing and drainage, then a healthy and sound horse doesn't need a foot of shavings in the entire stall. If a stable will allow you to bed your stall heavy, then you have found a place that suits your needs but it will come with an increased price tag. Remember what I said earlier, bedding will be one of the most expensive costs of any boarding stable and the barn owner is likely to establish strict rules about bedding for economic reasons.

25. Am I allowed to add extra shavings if my horse is hurt or has other issues?

This is an important question to ask. If your horse is severely injured or has an abscess or worse, laminitis, you are going to want to make sure the horse is as comfortable as possible, and the footing will play a part in this.

We have a mare at our barn that has a severe fungal infection and when the farrier needs to trim back the bad part of the hoof, it can be painful for the horse to stand on her feet. Her stall is bedded heavy, but the client pays for the extra bedding and will also come pick the stall at night since the horse is on stall rest. In this situation it works out well for everyone.

If the barn manager does not allow you to add extra shavings when your horse needs them due to a medical reason, then it probably is not the right barn for you. You might want to look further. There are so many variables in each situation that an in-depth discussion with the barn manager is warranted so you don't have frustration or regrets later if something happens to your horse and he needs to be on stall rest.

26. Is there an added fee if I would like a stall that is bedded heavier "just because"?

If you want your stall bedded heavier "just because" you feel it will be so much nicer for your horse, then you need to make sure they will do that at the stable you are looking at. In most cases there will be an added fee for the cost of shavings and the labor to clean a heavily bedded stall. Many stables will have a set amount of shavings that is allowed in each stall unless it is for a medical reason. If you want your horse's stall bedded heavier "just because" then you had better check first to see if they will approve it. Don't be disappointed if the barn manager says no to your request. At that point you will need to evaluate and decide how important heavy bedding is, especially if you absolutely love everything else about the barn.

27. Can I put toys in the stall for my horse?

You will want to ask if you can hang toys on the walls or have them on the ground. Many horse owners will purchase Jolly Balls and other things to entertain their horse while they are in their stall. A stable might be finicky about this so it is best to ask rather than making assumptions.

28. Do you supply salt/mineral blocks? Is there a fee? Can I supply my own?

Often a boarding stable will have salt block holders on the stall wall for salt or mineral blocks. You will want to ask if the stable supplies the blocks and how often. Some horses will hardly touch their salt or mineral block while others might eat it like candy. If your horse goes through a lot of salt blocks then you will want to ask if there is a limit per month. Our stable will supply salt blocks as part of the board rate but we do not supply mineral blocks. I have clients that will want one or the other and at times both! This is not a deal breaker but at least you know exactly what is included in the board.

29. Can I hang a fan on the stall during the hot summer months?

This is a great question to ask especially if you live in a hot and humid area. If the barn doesn't have good ventilation and air flow then it might turn into a hot box for the horses that are in stalls. Most barns will allow fans, but you will need to confirm what is acceptable. Also ask if there is an added monthly electrical fee to have the fans on.

Water – Super Important!

30. How often do you top off the water buckets in the stalls?

It is important that your horse have accessible water ALL the time and you will want to know how often the buckets are refilled especially if they are in their stall for a long span of time with only one bucket of water. I have provided some information below from the American Association of Equine Practitioners about normal water consumption for a horse.

A horse's daily water requirements are influenced by age; body condition; the amount, type and quality of feed consumed; fitness level; and activity level. Add to that the temperature, as well as the freshness, purity and palatability of the available water and it becomes obvious that there are a number of factors that influence water consumption. An idle, 1,100-pound horse in a cool environment will drink 6 to 10 gallons of water per day. That amount may increase to 15 gallons per day in a hot environment. Work horses require 10-18 gallons of water per day on average but could require much more in hot weather. Nursing mares drink more water because of fluid loss associated with milk production and increased consumption of feed to support milk production. A 1,100-pound nursing mare can easily drink up to 20 gallons of water per day. Foals also have higher water requirements and will drink 6 to 8 gallons of water per day even in relatively cool weather. A horse's water consumption will also be greatly affected by the temperature of the water. Consumption appears to be best when the water temperature is between 45 to 65 degrees Fahrenheit.

Information above from American Association of Equine Practitioners - https://aaep.org/horsehealth/cool-clear-water

31. Are the buckets heated in the wintertime so that the water doesn't freeze?

Horses should NOT have to break through ice to get a drink of water. This is something they may do in the wild out on the range but if you are paying a lot of money for someone to take care of your horse then that should include fresh (not frozen) water. Do most horses do okay if the water is extremely cold? Sure, most of them will do fine but what if you have a horse that has health issues and you need to make sure he is drinking a lot of water? Water helps keep their intestines and gut moving and it is a vital part of keeping a horse healthy. If you are looking for optimal care for the health and well-being for your horse, then having heated water buckets or water tanks is best during the months that the water will freeze. Don't compromise on water and the care of your horse.

32. How often to you check to make sure the automatic waterers are working correctly?

Automatic waterers are great and make life for the employees so much easier. But if the automatic waterers are not cleaned and maintained they can break and stop working. If no one is checking them daily, then a horse can be without water and that is not acceptable. There are many opinions about automatic waterers in the horse stalls. Some people like to physically see how much water each horse is drinking down daily when the horse is in his stall. For others it is not such a big deal and in most cases it is not. The important thing to take notice of is if the stable quickly fixes the things that are not working properly, and that includes the automatic waterers. If they do not check the automatic waterers daily to make sure they are working properly, then a horse could be without water for a very long period of time before anyone noticing and that is NOT good!

33. How often do you clean them?

Cleaning water buckets and water tanks is not fun but needs to be done consistently when they become dirty in order to keep your horse healthy. Much will depend on the weather and season. Our outdoor automatic waterers don't need cleaning as often in the cold of winter as in the hot humid days of summer. Common sense often determines how often buckets and water tanks should be cleaned. If you inspect them and they are full of algae or other crud then they need to be cleaned. If a stall bucket smells (especially if you have a horse that dunks his hay) then clean it. It is as simple as that. If a horse is gone for more than a day then the water bucket should be emptied until the horse returns. This ensures that the horse will have fresh clean water when he returns.

34. Do you clean them with water only or do you use a cleaner?

This may seem like a strange question to ask but I have seen all sorts of cleaners used to clean water buckets. Sometimes the smell of the cleaner is enough to knock you out! If the smell is that strong then there is a very good chance your horse will not like it either. Remember that they are sensitive to smells and just because we like that Clorox bleach clean smell doesn't mean they will! Most stables probably are not that particular when it comes to cleaning buckets and tanks, but it is something to be aware of, especially if your horse stops drinking.

Outside Board - Often referred to as "Rough Board"

Outside board or "rough board" is typically when the horse lives outside 24/7 with other horses and a shelter. There is no horse stall for them to come into at night and they are outside in all types of weather. For most horses this type of boarding works great. Outside board is usually less expensive than stall board because there is less labor and costs involved since there are no stalls to clean and bed daily.

If done right, outside board is a wonderful boarding option and can save the horse owner money. If done wrong, it can cost the horse owner more than they imagined in a stressed horse or even a vet call. Be smart when choosing outside board. Make sure it is a good fit for your horse, especially if you live in a climate that gets extremely cold in the wintertime.

I have listed a set of questions to ask when looking at outside boarding for your horse.

35. How many horses live together in rough board?

Asking this question in itself is not as important as how everything else is handled daily for the horses that are living together in the same paddock or pasture. A boarding stable can have many horses living together compatibly when everything is set-up in a safe and accommodating way for the living conditions of the horses including adequate access to water, food and shelter. At this type of stable you will be able to tell that the barn owner and manager are very strategic in how they do chores and the match-up of the herds. You can tour a stable and only see three horses living together in outdoor board but if it is set up poorly you are going to have issues between horses. In this situation one horse might be left out of the shelter or can't get to the food. **It's not the size of the herd as much as how the living conditions are set up for the horses AND it needs to be thoroughly considered and designed for all four seasons and all types of weather.**

Once you hear the number of horses for each grouping then you can start to ask the right questions to make sure that it will be a good fit for your horse. Remember that your horse will be living with other horses 24 hours a day, 7 days a week and 365 days a year in all types of weather! You want to make sure he feels very comfortable in his new surroundings because he will not get a reprieve from it or the other horses as stalled horses do when they come in each evening from their daily turnout.

36. Is there enough shelter for all of the horses to get out of the bad weather?

This is a very important question to ask because if there are too many horses living together for the size of the shelter then there is a very good chance some horses will not be able to get into the shelter during bad weather. This would include extremely hot days where they want to get out of the sun. If you are the owner of a timid horse who tends to be at the bottom of the pecking order then it can and will become stressful if you drive up to the stable and find your horse standing out of the shelter because he is afraid to get closer to the other horses.

This is where good herd management skills are important. A skilled and experienced barn manager will make sure there are accommodations for all the horses to get into a shelter without fear, whenever they want to. If a boarding stable is set up correctly then this is possible, and it works!

Now there are always those horses that love a good storm and will purposely stand outside in the middle of a storm. When a barn manager knows his horses well, he will be able to tell the difference between a horse that is standing out in the weather *just because he wants to,* and a horse that is nervous to come into the shelter because of fear. It is very easy to tell once you know the horses and understand horse behavior.

37. Can you explain to me how you handle extreme weather – extreme cold temperatures or bad storms?

When living in an area that has harsh winters and extreme weather you will want to ask the barn owner about alternative stabling and how they manage the horses during extreme negative temperatures or significant blizzards.

When considering outdoor board for your horse, you are going to want to educate yourself on the type of horse you have and how they will handle very cold temperatures. Most horses will do fine, while blanketing may be a necessity for the horse that might need a little more warmth during frigid temps. The truth is that some horses don't do well in extremely cold temperatures. Often very old horses or thin-skinned horses like the Thoroughbred or Saddlebred really struggle if the temperatures take a dive. This is why it is very important to understand the horse you own and also the area, weather and living conditions he will be living in. We would all love to have our horses outside 24/7 but the weather may not be suitable for all horses and can cause undue stress on them.

38. How do you feed hay for the outside boarded horses? Do you feed round bales or individual piles of hay?

This is one of those questions that I would rate at the top for importance. If your horse is going to be in a herd setting on outside board, then you will want to know how the stable feeds hay outside. There is no right way or wrong way but a large part of it will depend on the horses that are living and eating together. If the stable feeds large round bales and a few horses have to share a round bale, there will always be a more pronounced communication of who is in control of the food and which horse is allowed to eat. This sometimes doesn't work out well for the horse that is very timid, new to the herd or low horse in the herd. In this case, you might notice the horse starting to lose weight or become stressed if he is not allowed to get enough to eat. This is where a barn manager really needs to keep an eye on the herd and make sure all the horses can eat in a safe and secure setting with little stress.

If round bales are strategically placed in a couple of locations in the paddocks for the horses, there is a better chance that all the horses will be able to eat with less stress BUT it still is important that the herd is matched up evenly. The number of horses sharing a round bale is also important to note. Horses do not always share their food nicely and there needs to be other hay options if a horse is chased off a round bale.

Feeding individual piles of hay

Another way that a boarding stable will feed hay is in individual piles (enough piles so that every horse has one) that are set far apart so that every horse in the herd is able to eat. The horses will play "musical piles" as the top horse moves from one pile to another and then he moves all the other horses BUT they are still able to eat at a much more relaxed pace and they always have access to hay with much less stress. Even a dominant horse can only eat at one pile at a time and usually he will tire of moving other horses from one pile to the next as he settles into eating his food.

The one thing that is important and you need to think about is that a boarding stable will have horses leaving and new horses coming in as clients come and go. This means there will always be changes in the herds and with that comes the establishment of a new pecking order as the horses determine who is the top horse all the way down to the bottom. The established pecking order will show itself very clearly during eating time. This problem is more pronounced if a stable feeds large round bales to horses in a herd because the horses are in close proximity while eating and tend to become annoyed with each other and protective of their place on the bale. If your horse is always on top of the pecking order he will have no problem getting hay, but he could end up with a weight problem while another horse in the same herd may lose weight. Round bale feeding can present a less controlled way of feeding horses and can raise the risk of accidents or injured horses.

The way horses are fed can differ depending on where you live and the type of weather you have. In some areas of the country, horses are fed hay cubes instead of flakes of hay. It is something that is very important for you to find out as you tour stables and you want to make sure you feel comfortable with the feeding program, no matter where you take your horse.

Important note – Feeding round bales is an option if you have enough round bales so that EVERY horse can easily access food without stress. Some horses do not like to eat near other horses and this is something that you should observe so you understand your horse's eating habits and requirements. The other part to consider is the fact that when a stable feeds round bales so that the horses have hay all the time it may lead to obesity, which is now resulting in health issues for many horses. Horses get limited exercise, are overfed and consequently the weight epidemic is growing.

One last thing to think about – if a stable is feeding round bales for the horses and it is an area that rains a lot, the nutritional value of the hay will decrease and the rain could mold and ruin some of the hay. There are boarding stables that use covers over the round bales to keep the rain from hitting it and soaking into the bales and that is an effective way to keep the hay from becoming soaked and ruined.

We will discuss in greater detail the importance of how a stable provides hay in a later chapter.

39. How do you feed grain and supplements for the outside boarded horses?

Feeding grain and supplements for horses that are on outside board can prove challenging. When you are trying to feed a group of horses their portions of grain and supplements (which will be all different) in the same area, you are bound to have some problems. You will have slow eaters, fast eaters and horses that get very little grain and they will all compete for grain. It can be hard to keep them all at their respective grain buckets, especially if one of the horses figures out that another horse is fed sweet feed or something yummy like that. You will want to find out exactly how the stable handles this type of situation and how they ensure that your horse will get the grain and supplements you have paid for.

Often a boarding stable will pull certain horses out of their paddock and put them in a stall or separate area to eat their grain so that other horses can't get to it. If your horse is fed a lot of grain and is a slow eater then you will want to discuss this and find out what the options are.

40. Will you feed supplements and grain twice a day for the outside horses?

Boarding stables will offer grain and supplement feedings either once or twice a day. It doesn't mean one stable is better than the other because they feed grain twice a day to the outdoor boarded horses. It is just a personal preference for the barn owner and how he set up his chore routine for feeding the horses in his care.

It is important to ask if the stable feeds grain and supplements once or twice a day. It is done both ways and you don't want a surprise if you thought they fed twice a day and once your horse is moved, you find out the stable only feeds grain and supplements once a day! It happens often. I have been to many different stables and about fifty percent of the barns feed grain and supplements once a day for outdoor boarded horses. At my stable we only feed it once a day but many of the owners will come out in the evening to give their horse an evening grain feeding. You also might be able to ask the barn manager if they are willing to feed your horse an evening portion of grain. They might be willing to offer this extra service but there will probably be a service fee attached. It is just something to think about and it never hurts to ask.

We will discuss in greater detail the importance of how a stable feeds grain and supplements in a later chapter.

41. If my horse gets sick or hurt, is there a stall that he can stay in while he heals?

If you are looking at outside board for your horse, you will want to see if the stable has an open stall that is used for sick or injured horses. If your horse gets seriously hurt or is very sick and you don't have a stall to keep him in while he heals, you are going to become very stressed and your horse will too! Good care at a facility also means they have thought about the emergencies that happen with horses and are adequately prepared to care for a sick or injured horse.

42. How do you charge for outdoor boarded horses that are in rehab when using a stall? Who cleans the stall and provides the bedding?

If your horse is outdoor boarded but needs to use a stall for an extended period of time, you will want to ask the barn manager if they provide the bedding and if they will clean the stall. Every barn will do this a little differently and it depends on how they are set up. Some stables will only offer this service during emergency medical situations. Some stables will ask you to provide the bedding and you will be responsible for cleaning the stall and some will offer to clean and bed the stall for a fee. It is an extra service that is not a part of the amenities included with outdoor board so it would be normal to be charged for the service of cleaning and bedding the stall.

The Tack Room

If you love horses then you probably also love the smell of the tack room when you walk into it to grab your saddle and bridle or brush box. Every boarding stable will have a tack room but they will come in all shapes and sizes and the more you tour barns the more you will start to see a huge difference in how they are set up. The next set of questions are important to ask so that you don't have a surprise later when you move in and you find out that you don't have as much space as you assumed. The tack room is an important part of any boarding stable and how it is organized will tell you a lot about how the stable is run. Remember that every part of the boarding stable is connected and they all impact the organization and functionality of a well-run stable.

43. How many saddle racks will I get to use?

It is perfectly fine to ask how many saddle racks you will be provided. And it is a very important question especially if you own more than one saddle, which many people do. Many horse owners will ride both English and Western disciplines or have a work saddle and a show saddle. Some boarding stables will only offer one saddle rack per client while others have two or possibly three you can use. Ask questions at each facility because every stable you tour will do this differently.

44. How many bridle hooks do I get?

You will want to know where you can hang your bridles, halters and all the other fun stuff you will collect the longer you own horses. It will become very frustrating if you don't have anywhere to properly hang your bridles, lunge lines and other tools and equipment you use with your horse.

45. Does everyone get the same amount of space?

This is an important question! If a stable is well-run and equally fair to all its clients, then every boarder should have the same amount of space, saddle racks and bridle hooks. When this is not the case, it often leads to drama and even resentment from the client who feels like they are not getting the same amount as another boarder even though they pay the same amount in board each month. Take a special mental note of this as you tour each stable

46. Can I bring in a tack trunk?

You will want to ask if you can bring a tack trunk or other kind of storage container for all your other belongings. Fly sprays, ointments, brushes, leg wraps are only a small part of the things you will start to acquire and you are going to want a place to store them to help keep them clean and free from mice getting to them.

47. Is there a place to put my winter blankets?

If you live in an area that has cold weather, you might be blanketing your horse. If that is the case, there is a good chance you will have two or three blankets and you will need a place to store them. Sometimes blanket storage has been overlooked by the barn owner when they were designing their stable and then they realize they have limited room for blankets. You will want to find out where you can store your blankets so you don't have to keep them in the trunk of your car.

48. Is the tack room clean and organized?

A clean and organized tack room speaks volumes about the management of the stable. Look around and see how things are maintained and if the tack room is clean. Remember that a dirty tack room will attract mice and then you will really have a major problem!

49. Do you use dehumidifiers in the hot and humid weather so my leather won't mold on my saddles and bridles?

Ask if the stable puts dehumidifiers in the tack rooms during the hot and humid weather. Humidity can mold leather and will make everything feel damp. This is not good for all your expensive tack that you want to keep in good condition

Boarding Contract/Liability Waiver

50. Do you have a boarding contract?

A boarding contract is a necessity and it shows that the boarding stable is being run like a business with appropriate protections in place for both the barn owner and horse owner. The boarding contract should be clear and understandable and if you see something on it that doesn't make sense then you need to ask what it means and how it will affect you and your horse.   No two boarding contracts are the same and each stable will construct theirs according to what they offer as a stable.

51. Can I have a friend or family member come ride with me?

You will want to ask what the policy is for friends or family members to come ride or hang out at the barn. Most boarding stables will have liability waivers on site so you can have your friends and family fill it out and sign it before they handle or ride your horse. Remember that all visitors must always abide by the rules of the stable.

Barn Rules and Arena Rules

Barn rules are important for a well-run boarding stable and without a set of barn rules in place, you might become frustrated as you see people doing all sorts of things that are safety issues or disrespectful to other boarders. This is a very important part of touring a stable. Don't minimize the importance of barn rules.

52. Can I have a copy of your barn rules?

You can tell a lot about a boarding stable by the rules they have in place. The truth is many barns do not have or enforce barn rules and that is a sign that there might be chaos at times. Ask to see a copy of the barn rules so that you can read them and see if the rules will work for you. Some stables will seem stricter than others but realize that fair, consistently enforced rules are important for a well-run stable. Remember that the larger the facility the more people there will be at the stable and things can get out of hand fast if no rules are in place.

Another important consideration is whether the barn rules are enforced equally for all boarders. This will be something that you may need to ask other current boarders. It will become very frustrating if you follow the rules and you see others that do not and there is no accountability. A stable can have many rules but if they are not enforced fairly then you will have problems. There is nothing worse than a barn where the rules are not regarded as important and everyone is doing whatever they want. When you hear about a barn with drama, one of the leading reasons is – lack of enforcement of the barn rules.

It is also important to note that you may not understand all the rules listed. If you read a rule that you don't understand then ask what it means and how it will affect you. Every barn will have their own set of rules and they differ from place to place. If you find that too many of the rules will not work for you then the stable is probably not the right place for you. Don't expect the barn owner to change things because of your needs, likes or dislikes. They are a business and need to do what works best for them and their stable.

53. What are your barn hours?

As you look and tour boarding stables you are going to see a vast difference in barn hours. You will even find stables that don't have any hours. Ask what the barn hours are and then you can make a determination if those hours will work for you and your lifestyle.

54. What if I want to leave very early (before the barn opens) for a trail ride or horse show?

Most boarding stables allow the client to leave before the barn opens for travel with their horse. This is very common especially if they have to be somewhere early. Ask if this is allowed and what kind of notice the barn owner needs ahead of time so that there are no surprises when a truck and trailer pull into the stable at 4am! Great communication will play a huge part in this.

55. What if I won't be home until long after the barn closes?

When people go on trail rides or horse shows it is very common to arrive home very late in the evening, especially if they have traveled far. Make sure that late arrivals won't be a problem at the stable. In most cases it is not but you will want to check on how the barn manager wants to be notified when you are coming home after hours. They usually want to be notified so that they can make sure the stall is ready and hay and fresh water is provided for the horse. They also want to make sure the barn is closed properly after you leave and all the lights are out. This is something that they will discuss with you and instruct you on closing routines if you will be coming in after hours.

56. Can I see my horse after hours if he is sick and needs medical attention?

I have never heard of a barn owner or manager telling the owner of a horse that they can't come tend to his injuries or illness after hours BUT you never want to assume. I would ask just to make sure.

57. Can I bring my dog to the barn?

Dogs have always been a controversial subject for many boarding barns. Everyone loves to see dogs and horses together and many believe they go together BUT many dogs are not sufficiently trained and well-behaved and may challenge or chase other animals. It can become a huge liability for the barn owner if a dog bites someone and it will be tragic if the dog gets kicked and needs to be put down from its injuries. I have heard of both of these scenarios and both with a terrible ending.

You may want to bring your dog to the barn but if the barn owner has a rule of "no dogs on the property" then you will need to decide if you want to board at the stable. This is emotional for many people but if a barn has an excellent reputation for great care then leave the dog home and enjoy your horse! You can always see your puppy when you get back home.

Also, to defend the barn owner (since I am one), there is a very good chance that their business insurance will have a rate hike if they allow dogs on their property. Don't take it personally if your stable doesn't allow dogs. It has nothing to do with you at all. It is a horse business first.

58. Do I need to wear a helmet?

This is an important question to ask because each boarding stable will deal with helmets differently. Most stable owners/managers will recognize the importance of safe practices while riding and that will always include encouraging riders to wear helmets. Some barns will leave the question of helmet use entirely up to the rider or owner of the horse. It would be safe to say that most stables require children under the age of 18 to wear a helmet and if riders are jumping a helmet is routinely required. Enforcement of helmet rules can be challenging but you are likely to find that boarders help one another remember the importance of wearing helmets.

59. Do I need to wear boots at all times when handling or riding my horse?

This is one of those questions that will have a different answer depending on who you talk with. Most boarding stables will have a "proper footwear" rule, which means anytime you are riding you need to wear boots with a heel. It may be extremely hot and you may want to ride barefoot but you need to make sure you are within the guidelines of the stable. Many stables allow adults to make their own decision when it comes to riding or handling their horse but will enforce the rules for children under 18 years of age. I am a huge advocate for proper footwear while handling horses and riding and it is reflected in my barn rules but it doesn't mean everyone will follow those rules when I am not around.

I have witnessed the aftermath of a mother and daughter bringing their horses in from the pasture and both were in flip flops! The one horse stepped on the young girl's foot and crushed her toe with her mother holding the other horse. She had to be taken to the emergency room and she was in excruciating pain. She was lucky that she didn't lose her toe.

60. Can I drink alcohol at the barn?

If you like to have a drink at the barn with other people, then you need to make sure it is okay before you move your horse to the stable. Many stables allow alcohol at the barn and many do not. The same would be true for the person who doesn't drink and doesn't want to be around other riders who drink at the barn. The barn owner will need to decide what kind of barn they want to have and then they will attract those kinds of clients. It is a personal choice either way.

Horse trailer parking

61. Can I park my horse trailer on the property?

Having accessible horse trailer parking is a nice perk. Many stables will charge a fee to park your trailer on their property and others will not. It is a personal and financial choice for the barn owner and you will want to know the monthly cost if there is a fee.

62. Does every trailer have an assigned spot?

This may seem like a silly question unless you have boarded at a stable where you left for the day with your trailer and when you got home that evening or a couple of days later, your space was filled with another trailer and they were using your chocks! This scenario often happens so in order to alleviate drama and trailer issues, it is smart for the barn owner to assign spots for every trailer. This way if you are gone for a week of trail riding or horse show, you will have the same parking space upon your return.

I had purchased my first horse when I was in my early twenties and I was a very green rider and, to be very honest, horse care was the last thing on my mind. I didn't see the importance of checking stables and what they offer. The truth is, I thought they all pretty much offered the same thing.

I had bought a Thoroughbred who had come off the racetrack and had never been in a herd setting except when he was a yearling. On top of it, I lived in the upper Midwest where it becomes extremely cold and he was being shipped to me from Florida. Talk about a change! I wasn't even aware of how hard it would be on him physically.

I found a cute stable that I really liked and he was going to live on outdoor board with a shelter. That first winter was a huge awakening for me as I realized how cold he got and I didn't have blankets for him. I purchased a blanket right away without knowing what kind to buy. He was also having a very hard time adjusting in his paddock with all the other horses and his personality was changing in negative ways. I finally realized that outdoor board was not a good fit for him and the barn didn't offer stalls for horses, so I needed to look for a new place. I still feel terrible about those first few months and how stressful it was on my horse.

Since that first winter he has blossomed in a setting that is much better suited for him and he loves to go outside daily but is equally happy to come in each night. I have learned how to blanket him appropriately for the weather (with the help of the staff at my barn) and he is flourishing. I realize now how important the right living conditions are for each individual horse.

Susan

Chapter 3

Disciplines Matter When
Choosing a Boarding Stable

63. Is the stable a multi-discipline barn or one specific riding discipline only?

It is important to find out the riding disciplines of choice at the stable you are touring. You want to make sure the stable is a good fit for you and the type of riding you want to do. Most boarding stables will gravitate toward a couple types of disciplines and often it will depend on the trainers that work out of the barn. The footing of the arena will also play a part in what riding disciplines are common at a certain barn. For example – if the footing is not very deep, then the footing might not be good or safe for speed horses or reining horses. If the footing is too deep then it might not be appropriate for horses that pull carts and carriages.

If you tour a stable and you find out that everyone at the stable rides English and jumps or does dressage and you want to trail ride with other people then you might have a hard time finding someone to ride with. The people might all be very nice but you might struggle to find someone who wants to go out for a day or weekend on a trail ride. On the other hand you might be open to trying a new riding discipline and want to learn as much as you can. It is a personal preference and your goals and comfort level will help determine if the stable is a good fit for you and your horse.

64. How big is the riding arena for the type of discipline you plan on riding?

Size does matter for certain riding disciplines. Horses are big animals and need room to move properly and if the arena is too small then it can be hard on their body. Horses that are ridden continuously in a very small circle will often start to have back-end problems as they age. If all you have room for is small circles then it is going to become very boring very fast for both you and your horse.

Some riding disciplines don't take up a lot of room and the horse and rider don't need a lot of space but others require adequate space for proper movements. Really think about the riding discipline you plan on doing and the room you will need. If you are going to be jumping and plan on training on a full jump course in an arena then you are going to need room. If you are going to be setting up trail obstacles or pleasure riding then you won't need a lot of room.

65. How many riding arenas are there?

I often will be asked how many riding arenas we have at our barn. Many people don't feel comfortable riding outside an arena especially with a young horse and they want to have options. You might not like a crowded arena and want a stable that offers at least two riding arenas. Find out what the stable has for riding arena amenities and round pens and decide what works best for you.

66. How often is the arena dragged and maintained?

A great looking arena doesn't just happen. It takes frequent routine maintenance to keep the footing nice and safe for the horses. It is very appropriate to ask how often the arena is dragged. Walk in the arena and check the depth and composition of the footing. Take notice if there are a lot of rocks in it or if the footing has become uneven in many areas. If the footing is in bad condition, it can be hard on your horse as they move through it.

67. Can I set up jump standards or other types of equipment?

If you have equipment of any type then you will want to ask if it is okay to set it up when you are riding. Find out what the normal protocol is for setting up jump standards or other types of equipment that take up a lot of room. This is where a large arena can be important, especially with a large number of horses at the stable. Arena size vs. number of horses will play a part in safety and congestion when riding.

68. Is there a place to store my equipment?

If you have jump standards, poles, carts or other equipment then you are going to want to know if there is a place to store your things. Most stables will make accommodations for your equipment BUT it is better to ask then assume. It can be frustrating for the barn owner if they walk into the arena and find a whole bunch of jump standards or other equipment in a corner but were never asked if they can store them there. Out of courtesy for others it is best to ask first.

69. What is the busiest time of day in the arena?

You are going to want to ask about the busiest time of day at the stable especially when it comes to the riding arena. Arena availability and congestion can be very frustrating for people if they work a fixed schedule and only have a limited time to ride and that is during the busiest time of the day. After school and late afternoons are often the busiest arena times because kids are taking lessons or riding for fun. This is why it is important to ask about the size of the arena because if it is too small then you may have congestion and overcrowding if the stable has many horses and clients with similar schedules.

You need to remember that there will be people not only riding their horses but lunging them as well and lunging horses takes up a lot of room!

70. Do you ever have a problem with overcrowding and safety while riding?

Ask the barn manager if they have a problem with overcrowding or safety. It is very appropriate to ask and listen carefully to the answer. There are no guarantees that no one will ever get hurt but the number of injuries should be low. If the arena is often overcrowded then the risks of accidents increase. It should be mentioned though that other factors such as the type of riding, skill level, arena riding rules and common-sense safety that the riders are doing also can contribute to risks.

You can have a large arena and only two riders using it and still have safety issues if someone is doing something totally inappropriate and unsafe with their horse. A barn manager who runs an organized and well-run stable will have this under control and be very aware of clients who might have a lapse in judgement when riding or playing with their horse. They will be the one to keep the barn and others as safe as possible.

71. My horse is trained in a couple of disciplines and I want to change it up. How will the current stable I am boarding at accommodate my interest?

Sometimes a person will change up the disciplines of a horse (especially if the horse is trained in more than one riding discipline) and you still want to make sure it is a good fit for the current stable where your horse is boarded. For example – if your horse is trained both English and Western pleasure and now you want to teach the horse to drive a cart, you will need to find out if that is allowed and if your stable will be accommodating for cart storage. You also need to make sure there is enough room to drive a horse safely in the arena.

I didn't realize as a new horse owner that the riding discipline of my choice would make a difference at the stable where I was boarding my horse at.

I also didn't know that the size of the arena would play a huge part in congestion and time available to use the arena.

I was boarding at a beautiful facility with great care for my horse but I was a western pleasure rider and the stable was largely a hunter/jumper and dressage barn. The jumps were often set up in the arena for lessons and training and there really wasn't enough room to ride while other people were jumping. Plus I felt it was a safety issue due to the small size of the arena.

I found myself becoming frustrated and it wasn't the barn manager's fault at all. It was just the type of boarding stable I was at and I finally had to make a decision about the stable I wanted to board at. I started to look around the area and this time I was much more knowledgeable and prepared to ask about the riding discipline that dominated each stable and I also took a good look at the size of the riding arenas which I now know make a difference in how crowded they become.

I loved the stable I was at but I have long since moved to another fabulous barn that has a large group of western riders and the arena has more room to ride and practice. It was a good move for me.

Pat

Chapter 4

Trainers/Riding Instructors and How They Will Affect You as the Client

Quality horse trainers and riding instructors can be a huge asset to any boarding stable. Trainers can add so much to a boarding stable but you need to make sure they are the right fit for you and your horse. Not every horse trainer is the right trainer for your needs so you will need to do your homework to make sure they have the experience, communication skills and qualifications to work effectively with you. When looking for a trainer, ask around and get references. You won't regret it.

72. Do you allow any trainers/instructors to teach out of your barn or do I need use the specific trainers already here?

This is a big one! You will need to find out what a stable's policy is regarding trainers/instructors and how that will affect you. Some boarding stables have "house" trainers and do not allow outside trainers/instructors to come in and teach. Be aware of this because if you have a certain trainer you want to use and the barn won't allow it, then you will want to look elsewhere for a boarding stable.

Many boarding barns allow outside trainers to come in and teach or work with a horse but some disciplines or certain training practices may not be allowed. The barn owner also has the right to say no to a trainer coming in if the practices or techniques go against what the barn owner allows. Educate yourself and ask for references when looking for a trainer for you and your horse.

Really do your homework when searching for a trainer and barn. They go hand-in-hand and often a stable will recommend certain trainers. I would encourage you to watch a prospective trainer work with a horse and see how he treats the horse and the techniques he uses.

It is also important to find out if there is a policy about mandatory lessons or training for you and your horse. At some boarding stables they might have a policy that you must take a certain number of lessons monthly to board there. They could even require your horse to be in part-time or full-time training. This is something to be aware of and you will want to discuss it with the barn manager. For some people this works out perfectly because if they can't be at the barn often, they know their horse will be ridden so many days each week. But for others, this might not work if they do not want to be locked into a mandatory lesson or training program. Do your homework before you move your horse so you don't have regrets later.

73. Do I need to sign up to use the arena when a trainer is using it with other horses and riders?

This is a great question because at some barns the riding arena will be closed during lessons. You will want to find out if this is the case for the stable you are considering. This will become very frustrating if you work and only can ride between 5pm and 7pm weekly and the arena is closed for lessons during that time. It is important to find out how the stable handles lessons and arena utilization.

If the arena is large enough then usually an instructor can teach a lesson with no issues while others ride. This is again where the arena size is important with respect to how many people can ride in the arena safely at the same time.

Some boarding stables will have sign-up times on a posted board where everyone can see which trainer is teaching and on what days and times. This works out great for a stable with a smaller arena. It lets the other boarders know when there are free times to come out and ride ahead of time, so they don't drive all the way to the barn to find out they can't ride because of lessons.

I didn't realize that there was a difference between a training barn (with one head trainer) and a boarding barn. I also didn't realize when I took an available stall that my horse would need to be in partial training or I would need to be in the lesson program. It wasn't explained to me until I had already moved my horse to the facility and this came as quite a surprise!

I decided to take lessons for a while but was having a hard time connecting with the instructor and what he was trying to teach me. I also had some questions about the training techniques I was seeing used on other horses at the stable. I asked if I could bring in my own trainer but that was out of the question. I now understand why – because that is how the head trainer makes their living. It was a great set-up for the trainer but it wasn't for me.

After some research and talking with other horse owners outside the barn, I decided that the current stable and situation was not a good fit for me or my horse. It was stressful to tell the trainer that I was leaving but I needed to do what was best for me.

I have learned a lot from that first boarding experience and now I have specific questions I ask about barn policy on trainers and who I can personally use. There is a huge difference between a training barn and general boarding stable.

Diane

Chapter 5

Herd Turnout or Private Turnout

When you are looking for a boarding stable you are going to want to learn how they do daily turnout for the horses. If you tour ten different stables then it is likely that you will see ten different ways of doing daily turnout. This is where you need to really look closely at the set-up for the paddocks and private turnouts and be mindful of the herd groupings and sizes. A horse can become stressed easily if the herd is not a good fit for him and it is important that the barn manager is knowledgeable and attentive to horse behavior and continually monitors compatibility within the herds.

This will be one of the most important parts of touring any stable because it can make all the difference in how your horse adjusts to a new environment and whether your horse thrives or becomes stressed and introverted because of the herd he is placed in.

This next set of questions are some of the most important questions in this book and you will learn a lot about a stable by asking them as you tour the facility.

74. Do you hand-walk the horses outside each day?

If the horses are in stalls and going outside each morning for daily turnout you will want to know if the horses are hand walked out individually or if they are run out in groups. The same will be true for when they come back in each evening. There are many opinions on the practice of running horses to and from the stall to their paddocks and each stable will have their own way of doing things. The one thing to be aware of is the fact that if your horse is run to and from their stall each day, the risk of your horse getting hurt in the process increases, especially when it is with a group of other horses, as they are all very excited to get outside to eat or come back in at the end of the day.

I have talked with two different people whose horses were hurt badly because they were running back into their stalls in the evening. One horse fell and hurt his leg and the other one got hung up on something that was protruding out of the stall (because he didn't make the corner) and needed to have stitches. I am not here to criticize any stabling practices but I do want you, as the horse owner, to be aware of what can go wrong in an instant. The other downside of the horses running in and out daily is that it is hard to give the horse a really good look over to see if there are new cuts, abrasions or lameness issues, especially if the employees become hurried in the process.

When an employee hand walks the horses daily they can watch them for any signs of lameness and take a good look at the entire horse to make sure there are no new cuts, abrasions, personality changes or other issues that may be missed if the horse runs in and out of his stall. This daily individual evaluation of the horse's condition helps assure that any problems are caught early and managed before getting out of control. It is just something to be mindful of when looking for a stable for your horse.

One more thought – If you own a very quiet horse that doesn't get nervous or over-react then a stable where they let the horses run outside daily might work fine, and that is where you really need to know your horse's personality. BUT if you own a nervous horse that tends to be very reactive then a stable that runs the horses outside daily and back in at night will probably not be a good fit and your chances for injury will increase.

75.   Do you check each horse thoroughly both morning and evening to make sure they are not lame, hurt or sick?

Accidents can happen anytime with horses, even during the night when we are sleeping. It has surprised me a few times over the years to come out to the barn in the morning and find a new cut or abrasion or a horse with a swollen leg and completely lame. These are the same horses that I tucked into bed and turned off the lights the night before and they were perfectly fine!

It is important to find out if the staff at a stable will be looking over each horse every morning and then again in the evening. It would be safe to say that many boarding barns check the horses in their care twice a day but it is always best to hear it straight from the barn manager how they do this.

76. How big are the herd groups?

The design of the paddocks and pastures will be very different for every stable and this will include how many horses are together in each herd. Herd size is a concern because once a herd becomes large it can become overwhelming for some people (who are not confident in their horse skills) to go out to the paddock to get their horse. This can become even more intimidating if you are lacking confidence and all the other horses come towards you and your horse is at the bottom of the pecking order standing alone in the back! It happens more than you know and for some people it can become frightening.

If a herd size doesn't bother you then you may not care how big the herds are at a particular stable. If it makes you nervous then you will want to ask the barn manager how large the herd is that your horse will be in and if there is someone that can teach you how to safely get your horse out of the paddock.

Listen to the barn manager's answer and hopefully she has a heart of a teacher so that you can grow in your horsemanship skills and gain confidence in this area. If this is not an option then you might want to think about a stable that has smaller herd sizes that will be more manageable for you.

77. Do you separate mares from geldings or have mixed herds?

This is a great question as there are many different opinions about housing mares and geldings together. Each stable will handle this differently but what is more important than whether the horses are geldings or mares, is whether the barn manager and staff are knowledgeable at herd placement and management and recognize issues when they appear in a herd.

In all the years of running our boarding stable we have always had one herd on the property that is a mixed herd of geldings and mares. The key to a successful mixed herd is knowing which geldings can live with mares without acting "studdish". The same will be true for mares who lose their heads when they are around geldings.   It just depends on each individual horse. Some horses' personalities will change if they are put in with a horse of a different sex and watching the signs is important. Often, horses will do just fine in mixed herds and, if you watch closely, you will notice that the mares will usually run the show.

78. How do you introduce a new horse to a herd?

You will want to listen to the answer of this question very carefully. Introducing a new horse into a herd is always a heart pumping experience to some degree. As the barn manager, we watch and pay close attention to the squeals and other body language that could be normal or indicate impending problems. The risk of a horse getting hurt during the first couple of days in a new herd increases when they are still trying to figure out the hierarchy in their herd group. **This starts all over again every time a new horse comes into a herd and that is why it is great if the stable you are looking at has low turnover.**

I feel it is a "best practice" to make introductions gradually and NOT put the new horse into an established herd where he can become overwhelmed easily with every horse circling around him and running, kicking and so on. Instead I feel it is very effective to empty the paddock and put the new horse in the paddock to let him get his bearings, find the food and water and acclimate to his new surroundings. I think about the horses in his group and start off with the one I feel might be a good match. The goal is to find a herd buddy for him as quickly as possible.

There is no guarantee that horses won't kick or strike out at each other while introductions are being made but with fewer horses in the paddock you have a little more control over what is happening and you can pull out a horse easier if you need to. So much will depend on your horse's personality and if he is a dominant horse to begin with or if he is easy going and tends to get along with everyone.

The one thing I want to stress is that every stable will do this part of herd management differently and you really need to ask the right questions to find out how they will be introducing your horse into his prospective herd. If you don't like the practices of a potential stable when it comes to herd management then it is best to find another stable that is better suited for you and how they manage introductions of new horses.

79. What if it is not working out well for the new horse in a herd? Are you willing to move the horse to a different herd?

It is important to find out if the barn manager will move your horse if the herd he is placed in is not a good fit. Horses will kick and strike out occasionally but if it continues without ceasing and horses are getting hurt then that is a red flag. Does the stable have other herd options? This is where a well-designed layout of paddocks and pastures is so important, because flexibility is important in order to find the optimal herd placement to assure safety and comfort for each horse.

When a stable doesn't have the flexibility to move a horse then you might run into some problems as the horse may be physically injured or become stressed under these conditions and that could lead to other health concerns. It all goes together, so it is important to know what the stable options are for herd management.

80. Will you contact me if there is a problem with my horse?

Communication is so important and it shows in a well-run boarding stable. A stable that is organized and has great communication will contact the owner of a horse if they notice an issue of any kind. If a barn has a poor communication protocol and history, then I would take a closer look at how everything is run daily and realize that this could be an issue if your horse is sick or injured. Good and reliable communication is a key factor in the well-being of your horse and your ability to feel confident in the care your horse is receiving. The importance of this component of stable management cannot be overstated! Often you won't know if a barn has great communication unless you can get references (which I highly recommend) and ask current boarders what they have experienced.

81. Will someone contact me if my horse loses a shoe?

It will become very frustrating if you come out to the barn after missing a few days and plan on riding and you find out that your horse lost a shoe three days ago and no one contacted you to let you know. I believe it is common courtesy and part of running a good business to let your clients know if their horse has lost a shoe. Now to be honest, I have missed noticing a missing shoe once or twice over the last fifteen years and I felt terrible when the owner came out and couldn't ride. But as a barn owner and manager I try my hardest to notice everything about the horse when I bring them in daily and that includes loose or missing shoes.

82. How long are the horses turned outside each day?

This is a great question and you are going to want to know the answer! Every barn does this differently and it can make a difference for your horse. Some barns only turn horses out for a few hours each day as part of their standard routine while others leave them out long past dark. This will be a personal choice based on your preferences, locale and what you feel comfortable with for turnout for your horse.

Can you ask to modify the turnout for your horse? Yes you can, but don't be surprised if the barn owner says no. They have their stable routines set up in a manner that works best for them and if they are not willing to accommodate you then that is okay and you need to look for a stable that better suits the daily turnout needs for your horse. .

83. Are the horses turned out every day? What about in the case of bad weather? What about holidays?

Every stable will do turnout differently but most boarding stables like to get the horses out as much as possible because they understand that it is so much better for the horse both physically and mentally. It is also much more work when the horses are stuck inside their stalls for long periods of time. It is a good question to ask. Some stables will not turn out horses on Sundays and holidays.

You will want to know what the turnout protocol is for bad weather. Is the barn you are looking at conservative in that they keep the horses in during bad weather or do they turn them out regardless of what the weather is? You need to find a stable where you will be comfortable with how they manage daily turnout for your horse, so it is important to ASK first before you leave a deposit to hold the stall!

84. Do you offer semi-private or private turnout?

Many boarding stables offer semi-private (2 or 3 horses) and private (1 horse) turnout and if that is something you are looking for then ask what they have to offer. You also will need to know if they have any private or semi-private spots available. Sometimes they are full at the time and then you would need to be put on a waiting list until a spot opens for that type of turnout.

85. Is there a fee for private turnout?

It is very common for private turnout to have an added monthly fee. It is more work to accommodate a horse on private turnout. If you are planning on having your horse on private turnout year-round or during the show season then you will want to ask if the barn has availability for this and what the monthly cost is. Some places may not offer private turnout so you will want to be aware of this and factor it into your decision making.

86. What if I only want my horse to have 2 hours of turnout a day? Do you allow that?

If you are looking for a stable where your horse will have limited turnout then this question is an important one. Some stables will offer limited turnout while others don't. Some boarding stables want the horses outside all day and will not make exceptions for clients. Find out first if this is available before you say yes so you are not disappointed later.

87. Do you offer night turnout?

There are a few reasons why someone might want night turnout for their horse. Turnout decisions can be impacted by factors such as weather, insects, riding disciplines, show schedules and owner preferences, to name a few. If you want night turnout then you will need to ask if the stable offers this or is willing to accommodate you.

88. If the weather is nice, can I have my horse left outside 24-hours a day?

Some stables will allow owners to leave their horse outside 24-hours a day during nice weather. If this is something that you want for your horse then you will need to find out if the barn offers this. If a stable offers this service then there is a good chance your monthly board fee will **not** be pro-rated for the reduced use of the stall.

There are also some stables that will require horses to stay outside 24-hours a day during nice weather without an option to use the stall you are paying for. If this is a requirement of the stable you are looking at then you will really need to think about your horse and if this will cause undue stress on him. Some horses do fine with being outside 24-hours a day but if a horse is used to being stalled regularly and then you change things up and leave him out 24/7, he might become stressed. It will depend a lot on the horse. Some will settle in and others never do. This is where knowing your horse and his personality quite well will help in deciding the right stable for you both.

89. Will you bring the horses inside the stable early if the weather is extremely hot and humid?

This will be an important question for some because of the weather conditions in the area where they board. If you are looking for a stable where the horses are turned outside daily but there is no shelter, then you might want to ask about how they manage extremely hot temperatures during the summer. Often a stable will turn horses out early morning and if the weather is calling for a heatwave then they might bring the horses in midday to get them out of the sun. It depends on how they are set up and if they have shelters in their paddocks or not.

90. Do the horses have shelter outside?

It is common not to have shelters for horses that are turned out daily and then brought back into their stalls at night. Many boarding stables are not going to build shelters in their pastures for daily turnout; instead, they will do turnout daily depending on the weather. If you are looking at a stable that has shelters in the paddocks for daily turnout, then you will want to find out if the horses are turned out regardless of inclement weather. They might do turnout daily regardless because of the shelters in the paddocks or pastures.

The important thing to think about is — **Will your horse be able to utilize the shelter anytime he wants and is the shelter big enough to handle the number of horses and their personalities in the paddocks?** It won't help your horse in bad weather if he can't get into the shelter. I just wanted to give you something to really think about and discuss with the manager prior to making decisions. It will be worth your effort to also talk with some boarders to get their perspectives on how inclement weather impacts the horses.

91. How do you handle ice in the paddocks during the wintertime?

If there is ice in your horse's paddock then it is dangerous for the horse! Horses can fall or splay (when the legs slip out from underneath the horse in a split like fashion) on ice very easily and the outcome in usually not good. Ask how the stable handles ice during the wintertime. This is one of the most important questions you need to ask when looking at a boarding stable in an area where it freezes and snows.

92. How do you handle extreme muddy conditions in the paddocks during the fall and springtime?

Mud can be a real problem if you live in an area that gets a lot of rain. Drainage and soil composition plays a big part in the condition of the paddocks, especially during times of extremely rainy weather. The amount of mud a horse will have to deal with is sometimes beyond anyone's control, especially if it keeps raining and doesn't want to stop. This is probably one of the most frustrating parts of running a boarding stable as it impacts the employees, who are dealing with it daily, the barn owners who need to make decisions on how to manage the mud situation the best they can, the horse owners, and of course the horses. Mother Nature controls these conditions!

Sometimes a stable can do paddock improvements which could include taking off topsoil and adding a lot of dirt and other types of footing or put drain tiles in to help move water faster but the truth is most barn owners cannot afford the cost of those improvements, especially when it doesn't always resolve the problem. It may help but much will depend on the area (high or low land) and the type of soil.

As a horse owner you will need to decide how muddy paddocks will impact your horse and your life at a boarding stable. A little mud is not going to hurt a horse. They may get very dirty from rolling in it (which they love!) and it can become an annoyance for the person who loves a sparkling clean horse, but if you get past the cosmetics, a moderate amount of mud will not hurt them. Mud does become a concern if is too deep where they can pull tendons or are really struggling to walk through it. Common sense will play a part in all of it for both the barn manager and the horse owner. Many horses can be out in the mud and never have a problem with it and then one horse can go out in the mud for a short time and end up with Scratches or other skin irritations. It will depend on the horse.

As the owner of the horse, it is best to thoroughly discuss your concerns with the barn manager when you are touring the stable to make sure you feel comfortable with how they deal with the rainy season and mud. EVERY BARN WILL DEAL WITH THIS ISSUE IN A DIFFERENT WAY and you need to find a stable that you feel comfortable in their decisions when it comes to mud and your horse. If mud is a major concern then you might want to find a stable that is on higher ground or has invested the money to make sure the paddocks do not get too muddy. If a stable has invested a lot of money in soil drainage mitigation, then that may be reflected on their monthly board rates. It is certainly worth paying a higher monthly board rate to have your horse in footing that doesn't get very muddy and has reliable drainage.

93. Can my horse stay in when the paddocks are extremely muddy so he doesn't pull a shoe?

If your horse wears shoes, then mud can prove a nuisance when it is deep. If the soil is a clay soil and is starting to dry a bit, it can become thick and contribute to shoes pulling off. If you feel this will be a problem then you will want to ask if your horse can stay in until the paddocks dry enough so that you are not losing as many shoes. There are no guarantees either way. I have seen horses go out in mud and never lose a shoe and then I have had horses go out on dryer paddocks in the summertime and lose shoes. Much will depend on the type of shoes and the type of hoof your horse has and even how the farrier puts them on. A lot goes into the whole equation and it is often not just the mud that is the issue.

94. How often do you clean the paddocks (often called dry lots) outside?

Cleaning the dry lots is much different than cleaning stalls. Some barns may try to clean them daily by hand (with a wheelbarrow and pick) but for many larger stables, they will use a tractor or skid loader to scrape and clean the paddocks. Where you live and the type of weather you have will dictate how often the paddocks get cleaned and maintained. If the ground is frozen then it is realistically too hard to get all frozen (and I mean frozen to the ground!) poop off of the ground. Often it is best to wait until things start to thaw out a bit to scrape and remove manure. This can make things even more complicated when the ground becomes extremely soft during the spring thaw and the equipment is too heavy to drive into the paddocks. It will tear up the paddocks and often get stuck if the ground is too soft.

It is natural for the horse owner to want a clean and dry paddock for their horse but the horses will be just fine if paddocks are not cleaned daily, especially during the wet season or when things freeze up. Often the manure will decompose and break down before it can be removed, especially if you get a lot of rain. This is not the case in a warmer and dryer climate where the manure cannot break down as fast. In those areas the paddocks will need to be cleaned frequently to keep the flies and insects under control. A stable will often try to clean the paddocks the best they can but they are often at the mercy of the weather and season.

I owned horses on the west coast for years but when my family moved to a much colder climate, I was completely caught off guard about all the things to know when it comes to taking care of my horses.

I had not experienced frozen water tanks or buckets and I assumed that every boarding stable would make sure the water was not one big ice-cube. I found a stable that felt like a good fit but I didn't ask the right questions when it came to cold weather and water. It turned out that the water tanks were often frozen and I would see other boarders going out to the water tanks to break the ice off of the top so the horses could drink. This seemed like a normal practice for many but I didn't feel good about it at all for my horse.

I talked to the barn owner and asked him why they don't use water heaters in the water tanks and he told me that they never do and the horses do just fine. I went home that day and decided I needed to find a new boarding stable where I didn't have to worry about frozen water all winter.

After years of having my horses in a colder climate I have learned so much about the proper care for horses during all four seasons and water is always a top priority for me.

I would rather be at an older barn that isn't fancy or doesn't even have a bathroom as long as my horses have accessible fresh water (not frozen!) all year round. My horses care will always come first before my comfort.

Michelle

Chapter 6

Horses with Medical/Special Needs

When I was a little girl I thought that horses were so strong that nothing could hurt them. Now that I have grown up and run my own stable, I realize how vulnerable and fragile they truly are. If you are a new horse owner then you might be in for a surprise at how often horses can become lame, injured or even sick. They can have teeth issues that will make your dental appointments seem like nothing compared to what they may have to endure, especially as they age. They can have vision problems, emotional issues and most horses will develop special needs as they age.

Finding a boarding stable that will properly take care of a horse with medical needs can be tricky and learning the right questions to ask will help you determine if a stable is a good fit for your special horse. You need to remember that not all stables are equipped to manage every special horse or medical need and it will be up to the barn owner/manager to decide if they can offer the services your horse requires. Asking the right questions is the best way to find out.

95. My horse is a yearling. Do you offer any kind of special turnout for very young horses until they mature?

There is nothing sweeter than a yearling who is trying to learn new things and figure out his new life. Very young horses have a lot of growing up to do and they have their own special needs due to their age. It can become very dangerous for a very young horse to be placed into a large herd of adult horses that he has never known before. Often the adult horses will be hard on him and, in the process he could be hurt. It is a much better practice to put a very young horse in with suitable horses that he can play with but also learn from and that is something that has to be well thought out by the barn manager. Often an older horse can be a great teacher if the older horse is gentle and has that type of nurturing personality. But if you put a very young horse into a large herd of horses without any prior notice then he might have a huge struggle, especially if some of the horses tend to be aggressive.

Ask what kind of accommodations a stable can offer your young horse as he matures so that he can learn from a few horses while at the same time minimizing the risk of injury. The right older horse can make all the difference in the world for a very young horse that is learning.

96. Do you offer special turnout for the senior horse?

If you are the owner of a senior horse you need to understand that as he ages his needs are going to change. Looking for a stable that provides care for the aging horse can prove challenging at times. If you have a senior horse that has slowed down physically and is starting to develop other issues then you might want to have him live out his days in a smaller, quieter herd setting. You will want to ask what kind of accommodations the stable can provide for your senior horse and make sure it is a good fit with other horses.

97. Will you soak the hay for my horse?

If you have a senior horse with teeth issues or a horse with metabolic issues, there may come a time when you need to start soaking his hay and feeding him mash. This is something that does create more work for the stable and employees and you will want to ask if they can accommodate and provide this service. This type of care is often prescribed by an equine veterinarian and most stables will try their hardest to provide the proper care for a horse with these special needs. If your horse needs this type of care, then ask before you assume they will provide this kind of daily care. There also might be an added service fee depending on the amount of extra work involved.

98. My horse has ulcers and needs to be given ulcer medicine thirty minutes before he eats his grain and hay each morning. Can you provide this service?

Currently horse owners hear a lot about ulcers in horses and how common and dangerous this condition has become. If your horse has been found to have ulcers, then you might need to give him a daily ulcer medicine on a strict schedule. You will want to make sure that the stable is willing to follow the veterinarian protocol for giving ulcer medicine daily. If your horse is prone to ulcers and has had issues with colic, then your veterinarian may recommend using a hay net to slow the horse's eating so he keeps food in his belly and the gut active. You will want to ask the barn manager if, under these circumstances, they are willing to hang a slow feeder hay net for your horse. It can change things up a little in the feeding routine of the horse and it is important to find out how the stable will handle this special care.

99. My horse has vision problems and has a difficult time seeing outside – What accommodations can you offer?

Horses can get all kinds of vision problems and there may come a time when it is best for your horse to be alone or with only one other horse. Vision problems can pose extra work for the stable and usually they will try to set up an environment to help the horse thrive and not become stressed due to his poor eyesight. Talk to the stable you are considering and make sure they understand exactly what is going on with the horse and what the future will look like if his vision becomes worse. They may not be set up to handle a horse with vision problems, but they might be willing to change things around to help create a safe place for your horse.

I bought my horse, Chester when he was 10 years old and have boarded him ever since I have owned him. I was able to find a wonderful stable that fit my needs and more importantly took excellent care of him during those years when we were competing and going to shows every weekend during the summer months. As he started to age and become a senior horse, we stopped showing and we enjoyed trail rides and a much more relaxed routine, and I stayed at the same boarding stable during all those years.

It was very hard for me to realize that my guy started to age faster and needed special attention as his health needs changed. When he hit is late twenties he started to have teeth issues and it resulted in him needing his hay soaked and his grained soaked as well. He also slowed way down and needed a much quieter paddock with fewer horses. I asked the barn manager if we could change his living arrangement during the day when he was outside and only put him with one other older horse. I wanted him to stay at the stable but they were already fully occupied and had nowhere to go with him and one other horse.

I finally had to make a very hard decision and look for a new boarding stable where they could take care of all his special needs and I wouldn't have to worry at all. I was looking for a forever home until his last breath and I wanted to make his last years his best years.

I searched and found a quiet little boarding stable and after talking to the barn owner about all the special care Chester would need every day of the year, it turned out to be the perfect retirement home for Chester and he lived out is days in peace with another older gelding. It was the best move for him and me.

Melanie

Chapter 7

Hay, Grain and Services Offered

This is one of the most important chapters in this book because a barn can be beautiful on the outside but if they are not feeding good quality hay or enough of it then you are going to have issues. You will want to learn as much as you can about how a stable feeds hay, grain and supplements and how they feed it daily. You want to make sure your horse is not becoming stressed because he cannot get to the hay due to other more dominant horses in his herd or the stable is simply not feeding enough. It happens and you want to be aware of what to look for because it is a vital part of your horse's health and well-being.

We touched a little bit on feeding hay and grain for "outdoor boarded horses" in a previous chapter but this chapter will go into much more detail about how the feeding program is set up at boarding stables. Remember that each barn will set up their daily feeding program differently. The more you can educate yourself on feeding and nutrition the better you will be equipped to know what to look for when you tour a boarding stable.

100. What type of hay do you feed?

It can be important to look at the hay being fed at each stable you visit. You should feel very comfortable inquiring about the type of hay, the hay supplier, hay quality and the feeding routines. The owner/manager should be cooperative and welcome your questions. Look for answers that are clear and understandable. There are many different opinions on hay, hay quality and how to feed hay. It can get crazy fast if you allow it to consume you. Not every horse needs heavy

Alfalfa hay and a good grass mix hay is perfect for most horses. If your horse has health issues, then you will want to talk to your veterinarian to find out if a certain type of hay would be best for your horse. The thing you want to understand is that not every boarding stable is going to offer an assortment of different types of hay to feed. Most horses do fantastic on a good quality grass hay or grass mix as long as it is mold free. If you are requesting special hay and the stable is willing to feed it then be prepared because it will probably come with an extra fee for the special hay. If the barn will not feed a certain type of hay for your horse then you will want to look for a stable that will better fit your horse's nutritional needs.

I encourage you to learn as much as you can about hay and the different types of hay. There are many great equine books on feeding horses that will give you a great education on feeding hay and they were written by experts in the industry. You can also check around your area to see if the local feed store has an equine nutritionist on staff to answer your nutritional needs. There are also great Facebook equine groups that are focused on health and nutrition and you can learn a lot in those groups. The one thing to be aware of is that every person will have a different opinion and at the end of the day you need to do what is nutritionally best for your horse.

101. How much hay do you feed per feeding?

This is a very good question and you will want to listen carefully to the answer. If the stable will only feed "2 flakes" of hay and you have a large draft, warmblood or other type of very large horse then you are probably going to see your horse lose weight. If the barn will feed as much as is needed to keep an optimum weight on your horse then that is a good practice. Every stable does it differently and some will feed unlimited hay while others will feed a limited amount and charge a fee for extra hay that is fed daily. The size of your horse, his age, breed, how much exercise he is getting daily and if he is an easy keeper or hard keeper will play a large part in his feeding program.

It is important to understand that hay will be the highest monthly expense at a boarding stable (next to the monthly business mortgage if there is one) and the barn owner needs to make sure he is not losing money. This will often reflect in his monthly board prices or an added fee for additional hay.

102. If my horse is young and growing or underweight will you feed extra hay to help put on weight?

If you have just purchased a 2-year-old horse you should anticipate a few years ahead of growth spurts so feeding extra hay will be a part of making sure he stays nutritionally sound to grow big and strong. It is important to find out how the stable handles horses that need to have extra hay and calorie intake and if they are willing to adjust the amount of hay for your youngster. If a stable is not willing to do this then you will want to look for another boarding facility.

103. Can I have 1 flake of alfalfa and 2 flakes of grass hay per feeding?

Some boarding stables will offer different choices in hay per feeding. If you are looking at a stable that offers this specialty feeding program then find out exactly how they do this during the morning and evening feedings. If your horse is outside during the day with other horses how do they accommodate that? Things can become very complicated when a stable is feeding an assortment of hay at one feeding. You will want to find out how they manage this routine daily, especially if you are paying for a specific type of hay during each feeding. What if they run out of one specific type of hay? Is there an extra fee for this type of specialty feeding of hay? These are questions that might be of value if you are requesting a special feeding program for your horse.

104. Can I bring my own hay and feed it?

There are boarding stables that will allow you to bring your own hay and feed it and some will even offer a discount on board in this type of situation. I will have to say that it is not the norm but if you are looking for that option, you will find it in a "self-care" or "co-op" type of boarding stable. You need to ask the barn owner if they allow this and how it works at their stable.

Occasionally a barn owner will allow a boarder to bring their own hay and feed it in addition to the hay that is already being fed. This needs to be discussed and agreed upon in detail so it doesn't cause issues down the road with hay storage or the chance that someone at the barn might use the wrong hay when feeding all the horses. It is easy to get things mixed up when many people are bringing in their own hay. That is one of the reasons why many boarding stables don't allow that practice. Things can get out of hand quickly if you have a problem with people who are using another client's personal hay. Another problem with this type of program is that many stables just don't have the extra storage room for more hay then what they already supply.

105. Do you allow hay nets in the stalls?

There are different opinions on hay nets and slow feeders and it is completely up to the boarding stable if they will allow hay nets in a stall for a horse. Some barns have hay nets in all the stalls while many do not. It is a personal choice of the barn owner because it does create more work for the employees. If you are insistent on a hay net or slow feeder then you need to find a stable that allows for hanging one in the stall.

106. Can I grab extra hay if my horse is out of hay?

Grabbing extra hay for your horse to eat because they are out of hay is something that is frowned upon at many stables only because it gets out of hand by people who panic that their horse will not have hay in his stall. Hay is expensive and sometimes a person will grab too much hay and then their horse will waste it simply because they are full. Some barns will allow you to provide more hay as long as you are not putting a whole bale in the stall while others will have a strict "no touch" policy. Ask before you take hay and find out what rule is for putting more hay in your horse's stall.

107. Do you feed hay 2 or 3 times a day?

Boarding stables will usually offer hay feeding 2 or 3 times a day for horses in their care. Some stables will feed breakfast then give a "snack" of hay at noon and then an evening feeding of hay. There are many opinions about hay and how often a horse should be fed, but the determining factor is how much hay the stable is putting out for each horse during the feeding times and all four seasons will play a part in it.

It is always good to look around the stable at the horses and see what they look like physically and if they look healthy and in good condition. If a barn feeds twice a day, that is perfectly fine as long as they are feeding enough hay (good quality hay) so that the horses are not going for many long hours without hay during their most active time of day. Many stables feed only twice a day and the horses do great and keep their weight up throughout all four seasons. The hay is adjusted and increased in the wintertime since the horses will be burning more calories trying to stay warm. They also are not on pasture grass during the winter, so it is important to adjust the hay accordingly.

It is a personal preference but I don't think feeding 2 or 3 times a day should make a difference in choosing a barn as long as you know the horses are getting a plentiful supply of hay during the morning and evening feedings. If a stable feeds 3 times a day then it would of course make my horse happy, but it would not be the reason why I chose that stable.

If your horse has stomach issues (for example – an ulcer) then you will want to discuss this with the stable and see if they will modify their feeding program for your horse so he has some food in his stomach most of the time. Often a hay net can be used in the stall to slow down the horse's consumption yet allow for an active digestive system throughout the day and night. So much goes into the whole equation and that is why it is important to really know as much about your horse as possible regarding his health and equally important to know how much a stable is really feeding per horse. You will have a lot of homework to do!

If a stable offers hay feedings 3 times a day then that would require someone on staff to feed the horses a midday feeding. This could mean that more money is paid out to employees and that may be adjusted in the monthly board rate. Please remember that boarding stables are a business and the barn owner is not in business to lose money. If they don't run it efficiently as a business they will not be in business for very long. IT ALL ADDS UP.

108. Do the horses eat hay in their stall before being turned out for the day?

Some boarding stables will feed the horses hay in their stall and then turn them out a couple of hours later. I don't believe this is the norm, but you will see it from time to time. If the horses are fed hay in their stalls before they go out you should ask the question: **If the horses go out and haven't finished their breakfast, will there be more hay outside for them to eat?**

Each horse will eat at a different pace and some horses will eat fast while others eat slowly. Some horses will eat, then stop for a while and then start back up after they have had a little rest. Every horse is different when it comes to eating their hay and you can't make them eat faster or on the barn's timetable.

You don't want your horse to miss out on his full breakfast if he didn't have time to finish his hay when it is time to be taken outside for the day - **especially if no extra hay is outside for him to eat.** It can lead to stress and other possible health issues if he is not getting the proper amount of hay because he is a slow or intermittent eater.

109. Do you use round bales or individual piles for each horse on daily turnout?

You will want to listen closely to how the stable feeds hay when the horses go outside for the day. There are many ways a boarding stable will put hay out for the horses and that is not as important as how equally matched the horses are in the herds. If the stable feeds round bales and it is expected that all the horses in a

92

herd eat off of one round bale then there might be an issue (Okay, the truth is there will be an issue) with the horses that are on the bottom of the pecking order for that herd. They will probably have to wait it out until they feel it is safe to eat or they will take quick bites and pull away for a few minutes. This kind of "eat and flee" reaction can cause stress and weight loss in some horses and an unhealthy weight gain in the overeaters who are at the top of the herd and never stop eating no matter how much hay is in the paddock. It is not the ideal situation.

If a stable has several round bales per herd then it is a much better set up for the horses to rotate and settle in to eat. In this case most horses will be able to get to the hay but you may still have a problem if your horse tends to be overweight and is constantly eating. You will want to consult your veterinarian if you have a horse that is overweight and discuss possible options to help your horse maintain a healthy weight.

One more thing to think about when looking at boarding stables that feed large round bales is that the hay may get rained on and the hay quality will start to decrease. When feeding round bales there is often a lot of waste and the overall quality diminishes over time. Some stables will put tall covers or protection over the round bales, which is a huge plus in keeping the hay from constantly getting rained on, especially if you live in an area where it rains a lot.

A boarding stable that feeds individual piles of hay for all the horses in a herd will find that they will have less aggressive behavior between horses and the horses will move more as they rotate piles. The reason I find this way of feeding optimal for horse herds is because the horses become less stressed when trying to eat and are not forced to wait until "allowed" to eat. They always have food available even if they are walking from one pile to the next. It also gives the horses exercise!

If a horse is stressed at feeding time then it could affect his personality and performance especially if he is not getting enough to eat because he is low in the herd order and the other horses are not allowing him to eat. The way a boarding stable provides feed for the horses is one of the most important factors impacting the horses' overall health and well-being.

110.   Are you open to moving my horse if he is not able to get enough hay due to being at the bottom of the herd?

This is an important question especially if the stable you are considering feeds rounds bales. Ask the barn manager what they do in a situation where a horse is losing weight because he cannot get enough food to eat. Ask if they are willing to move your horse to a different herd if this becomes a problem. Find out how flexible the barn manager is in dealing with a serious issue like this. This is where flexibility and many paddocks will give the barn manager options when they need to move a horse and correct a situation. If you can, ask other boarders or get references when finding out how a stable truly operates and that includes the daily feeding of the horses.

111. What if my horse is overweight?

If your horse is overweight and you are concerned about him having unlimited access to round bales of hay then you will want to ask if the stable can make other arrangements for your horse. If the barn manager doesn't have other options then you will need to look for a different stable for the benefit of your horse's health. There is an epidemic of overweight horses today and you will have long term health issues unless you are able to get his weight under control. I cannot stress how important it is to find out how a boarding stable feeds the horses at each stable you tour.

112. Is grain included in the price of board?

Every stable will have a unique way of dealing with grain as part of their feeding program. Many will include a "barn" grain in the price of the board while others will not. **Don't choose a boarding stable just because the grain is included!** You need to look at the entire picture. If a boarding stable includes grain, then you will want to know the type of grain they include and how much they feed per horse. What if your horse doesn't eat the type of grain that the barn feeds? What if your horse only gets a small amount of grain but now you are paying the same price as a boarder that is getting six pounds of grain for her horse every day? Will you get a discount if you are not utilizing the grain provided by the barn?

Just remember that something can sound so good on paper or a website but if it can't be used by your horse then you are paying too much for something you don't need. On top of it, you are now spending more money to buy the type of grain your horse does eat.

113. What type of grain does the stable provide?

Ask to see the type of grain a stable will provide. Many boarding stables will offer 2 or 3 types of grain and they will only charge you for the amount your horse eats monthly. This type of system is a plus for the boarder because they have options and they don't have to run and pick up the bags of grain each month. However, when your horse has metabolic issues, needs to gain weight or lose weight or is a senior horse, the different grain options a stable offers might not be the best choice for your horse.

114. Can I feed my own type of grain?

It is important to ask if you can supply your preferred type of grain. Most stables will allow you to bring in your own grain. They might require you to bring in a specific type of garbage can or storage container for the grain. You will need to ask what they require and ask to see how other boarders have done it when bringing in their own grain. While most stables will notify you when your grain is getting low (as a courtesy reminder), remember that they have many horses to care for and at times they might forget to remind you that you need more feed. It happens at the best of stables so I would encourage you to make it your responsibility to ask the barn manager or look yourself when you think you might be getting low.

Another special note - If you have just purchased a new horse then you might not know exactly how much grain he will need daily to keep him at an optimal weight. This is where effective communication between you and the barn manager is important especially for the first couple of months as your horse settles in. You might start off feeding 2 pounds of grain a day and then modify it up or down, depending on many variables. Your horse's age, amount of exercise he gets daily, quantity of good quality hay he is eating and how he is settling into his new home also plays a part. Be ready for some grain changes during the first couple of months as you learn more about your horse and your new boarding stable.

115. Do you feed grain and supplements twice a day for "stall boarded" horses?

Most boarding stables will feed grain and supplements twice a day for horses that have a stall, but you never want to assume. Ask about their feeding program so that you are not surprised later if they don't feed grain twice a day.

116. What is the daily routine for feeding grain and supplements?

Ask the barn manager what their daily routine is for feeding grain and supplements. If your horse is stalled then they will probably feed your horse his grain and supplements in his grain feeder in his stall. This is usually before he is taken outside for the day. Often the grain and supplements are dumped in the feeder and are waiting along with your horse's hay when he comes back in for night. It is always best to ask about the stable's feeding routine so you get a sound understanding of how things are done.

117. Will you feed multiple supplements for my horse?

There are many different supplements on the market for horses and you may be feeding your horse 1 or 2 different kinds. You will want to ask the stable if they will feed the supplements you have for your horse and if they are willing to feed it twice a day. Ask them exactly how they do this as part of their daily feeding program. Most boarding stables will offer this service but will require you to combine your supplements into either baggies or containers to make it easier and less time consuming for the employees. They may want you to label each container with your horse's name or have them all in a large container of some type.

118. Will you feed an oil supplement for my horse?

If your horse needs to put on weight it is often recommended to add oil daily to his grain. You will want to ask if the stable will provide this service. Some do and others will not because adding oil is messy, attracts flies and it freezes in the winter if the barn is not heated and the temperature drops below freezing. Many stables don't want to hassle with it. The good news is that there are many wonderful fat supplements on the market so you should be able to find a different kind of fat supplement to add to your horse's daily diet. This is wonderful news, especially if you like the boarding stable and want to move your horse there but they don't feed oils of any kind.

119. Will you soak my grain for my horse?

As your horse ages or has teeth issues you might need to soak his grain or other food like beet pulp. If this is something that your horse requires you will need to make sure the stable can provide this service. It is also important to ask if there is an extra fee for this service. Every stable is different when it comes to special services regarding grain and supplements.

Pasture feeding

Summertime is always the best time of year for the horse owner especially when the horses are on pasture. There is a comfort in watching horses lazily graze in green fields of luscious grass - if you are lucky enough to live in an area that has pastures. Even if a boarding stable has pasture turnout it is important to ask the right questions to make sure it is a right fit for your horse.

120. When do the horses typically go out on pasture for the summer months?

If you live in an area that has pasture land it is a huge benefit for your horse! Potential clients who are on a tour will often ask about when we start putting horses out on grass for the summer. Everyone anticipates pasture turnout with excitement, especially after a long winter. Once the grass greens up and starts growing at an accelerated rate, everyone wants to see their horse running down the pasture having the time of their life.

Depending on where you live the season may be very short and to preserve the grasses, the horses may not go out on the grass until it is a foot long. Part of the whole equation has to do with smart pasture management in order to maintain the pasture for many years to come. Re-seeding the pastures because of overgrazing will take the pasture out of commission until it is re-established (which can take a couple of years) and will cost a lot of money, so managing the pastures to prevent destruction is very important.

If you are choosing a stable mainly because of the turnout on large pastures each summer, then asking when the horses go out on grass is an appropriate question. Please remember that the timing decisions will be dependent on weather, drainage and how wet the pastures are and, of course, the size of the pastures and herd size on each pasture. It all plays an important part in pasture turnout and management.

121. How do you introduce horses to grass in the spring?

It is important to find out how the barn manager will introduce the horses to grass in the springtime. If a horse is turned out on young growing grasses for too long and too fast, then they possibly can become sick and in worse cases develop laminitis. It is important to make sure the person in charge of introducing horses to grass knows what they are doing. Ask the barn manager how they introduce horses to grass and what the time limit is for the first couple of weeks of pasture turnout. Early grasses have a very high sugar content so knowledgeable management of pasture time is critical to maintaining healthy horses.

122. How long are they typically on grass during the day?

I am often asked how many hours the horses are on grass daily during the summer months. Some people would love to have their horses on grass the entire day while others only want their horse on grass for a few hours. As a barn manager it can get crazy trying to please everyone, especially with almost forty horses to care for daily. **As a horse owner you can ask this question and you will receive an answer but if it is not what you had hoped for, then the stable might not be the right one for you UNLESS you are willing to adjust your expectations. Ask yourself the question: Is pasture time the main focus and reason for choosing a boarding stable?**

Overweight horses may require special accommodations to keep their weight from increasing while on pasture. It is important to discuss weight management and pasture feeding with the barn manager. Many decisions will be dependent on the size of the pastures and how much edible grass is available. When the pastures are small for the number of horses on them then you might not have an issue. If the pastures are large with plentiful grasses you might need something different for the overweight horse (limited time on pasture, grazing muzzle, etc.).

123. Will you put a grazing muzzle on my horse when they are on pasture grass? Is there a fee for this?

If your horse needs a grazing muzzle when on pasture then you need to ask if the stable will manage putting one on him and taking it off daily. Most stables will offer this service but ask the question and don't assume. Ask first – it is better to be safe than sorry. Also, there might be a fee for this added service and every stable will be different in how they handle this.

124. Do you also feed regular hay both morning and evening with the horses being on grass all day?

Feeding hay while horses are on pasture grass will be entirely dependent on how much good quality pasture grass the horses have access to. This is done so differently at stables because of the many variables that need to be considered. It is important to see how the horses are maintaining their weight and adjust their feeding program accordingly. If your horse is losing weight because he is not getting enough pasture grass because of depletion of the pasture, then you are going to want to talk to the barn manager to adjust the situation. Talk to them about this scenario and ask them how they modify a feeding program in this situation. Horses are huge animals and they need a lot of forage to maintain their weight while a pasture only has so much grass on it to feed a herd of horses. Often a boarding stable will keep much of their land to grow and make hay for the horses so their horse pastures may be smaller.

125. Do the horses stay outside longer during the summer months?

This is a very normal question to ask and you will get many different answers. Many stables will keep the horses out longer in the summer while others will keep their turnout routine the same year-round. Some stables might not have a set schedule and the horses are brought in at different times depending on the day, the weather or events taking place.

I was looking for a stable that would have pasture turnout during the summer months. In my area it is common for many barns to have night turnout as an option but I wanted my horse outside during the day and in his stall at night. I had chosen a stable that offered both types of turnout and it felt like a good fit for my horse.

The one question I forgot to ask is how many hours a day will my horse be turned outside during the day. It turned out that due to the change in employees and shifts, my horse came in earlier than I expected which meant he was left in his stall much longer than I preferred. When I asked if we could extend the time he was outside during the day, they told me that it was not an option since they only had so many paddocks and had to switch all the horses for the night turnout group to go outside. The night turnout horses were outside much longer than the day turnout horses and I had never thought to ask about this.

At this point I felt this was not a good fit for my horse anymore because I didn't want him in his stall for such a lengthy period of time. I decided it was time to look around and find a better fit for him and what I wanted in a boarding stable.

I never dreamed that I needed to be so aware of how a stable operates when it comes to day and night turnout but I have learned from that one boarding situation and now I know the right questions to ask so that my horse has optimal turnout daily.

Carol

Chapter 8

Full Care vs. Partial Care and What That Looks Like

Full Care and Partial Care are two different types of boarding options and you will quickly find out that the services can vary from one stable to the next. Even if a stable says they offer "full care" you will need to do a little digging to find out what exactly is included in full care boarding. The same is true for partial care. Asking the right questions will be important to find out exactly what is included in the daily care.

Usually full care will include hay, water, turnout and cleaning the stalls but you will still need to confirm with each place you tour. Some boarding stables will advertise "full care" and they will include blanketing, holding for farrier and vet calls and even putting on fly spray or special requests at no extra fee. Partial care might mean that you need to supply your own hay or you need to clean your own stalls. It really is up to the boarding stable to define what they will offer for care and services and they can decide from there what kind of boarding stable they want to call themselves. One boarding stable's vision and definition of full care may be much different than another stable and it may differ depending on the part of the area and country in which you live.

126. What is the monthly board rate and what is included with it?

THIS IS THE BIG QUESTION! What is the cost of the monthly board? This is a question you will want to ask long before you come for a tour but don't let the price tag scare you, even if it seems a little higher than what you had planned on paying. You are going to really start to learn what components of care **create true quality care** and you can't put a price tag on that. Cheaper isn't always better and when it comes to horses it can be a disaster if you are not careful.

127. What services do you offer with full care?

Ask for a list of what is included with the board and full care. Before you go to your first stable, make a list (after reading this book) of the amenities that are important to you. Every horse owner is looking for something a little different in a boarding stable and you want to find a place that provides excellent care and an environment where you feel comfortable with how they do things.

There are many extra services that a stable may offer and some will include those services as part of the board – BUT BEWARE, YOU MIGHT BE PAYING FOR SERVICES YOU NEVER USE! If you are never going to blanket your horse and that is part of the services offered then you might be paying a higher board rate because the barn owner has invested time, labor and cost of employees for all the blanketing that is done. I personally like a stable that offers "a la carte" for the extra services they offer and what you pay for. This gives the boarder a choice about what they want to pay for and what they will do themselves or tag team with another boarder. Usually at this type of stable the board might be a little less than a stable that has the same amenities but also has included all the services as part of the board. Are you starting to get the picture? It is something to really take note of as you tour boarding stables.

128. Do you put on/take off fly mask and fly sheets? Is there a fee?

If your horse is going to need a fly mask or fly sheet then find out if they will put it on daily and if there is a fee. If you can't make it to the barn often then you will want to ask if they are willing to wash the fly mask if it becomes muddy after a rain and your horse has rolled in the mud. You don't want the fly mask to block his vision at all.

Some horse owners will leave the fly sheet on all the time since most of them are made of a light weight material and just have the fly mask removed each evening when the horse comes back inside for the night.

129. Do you put on fly spray or sunscreen?

If you want your horse to have fly spray put on daily then you need to find out if the stable will offer this service when you can't make it out. Sunscreen is something that most horse owners don't think about until they have a horse with a white muzzle or snip that seems to get sunburned especially around the nostrils. If you have a horse with sensitive skin then you will need to find out if the stable will put on sunscreen during the summer months. Again, this is where you will want to find out if there is a fee for this service.

130. Will you put on bell boots, splint boots or easy boots daily?

Most boarding stables have a standard list of services they will provide for an extra fee and then there may be a few things that are TBD or To Be Determined. Putting special boots on daily can be easy or it can be extremely challenging depending on the horse, the boots and the conditions.   What can make it even more work is when you bring the horse back in from outside and he was in the mud and now the bell boots or easy boots are muddy and need to be hosed off otherwise the Velcro will not stick the next day. It can become more work than a barn manager anticipated at first and this is why they may decide to add a fee.

131. Do you have an "Extra Services" price sheet?

Ask the barn manager for a copy of their "Extra Services" price sheet so you can look it over and see what they offer as part of the board and what services will cost you extra each month. Becoming educated in how boarding stables operate will help you become more aware of hidden fees that could catch you off guard at the end of the month when you receive your invoice. A well-run boarding stable will make things very clear to you so that you don't have any surprises each month and you can then budget for your expenses and enjoy your horse!

 *When I was looking for a boarding stable for my horse I was still a fairly new horse owner and had very limited knowledge of how boarding stables operate. I just assumed they were all pretty much the same.*

I chose a stable (which was more expensive than some of the other stables in the area) and didn't think to look at what they really offered for services as part of the board fee. It took me a few months to figure out that I was paying a lot of money for many services I didn't use.

Many of the boarders at the same stable had their horse blanketed daily and this was a service that was included in the board. They also included the service of "holding fee" for the farrier but I was able to be there for all my vet and farrier appointments and really didn't need that service.

Another service I was paying for that I didn't use was the grain that was included in the board. They fed one specific type of grain and allowed up to 6 lbs. of grain daily as part of the board. It was great for the horses that needed a lot of grain but my horse was a very easy keeper and didn't get grain or if he did, I fed him a different type that was very low fat and I bought it myself.

During our time at this stable I changed jobs and got married. My new job was much better in many ways but I took a pay cut. I needed to think about my lifestyle and the extra money I was spending and decided I was spending too much for monthly services I never used the entire time I was at this barn.

I decided to talk with the barn owner and see if they would do a separate rate (decrease board rate) for the boarders who didn't use these special services. They only had one option in all the time I was there and it was worth a shot asking. Much to my disappointment the barn owner wasn't interested in changing how he did things so I decided it was time to look elsewhere. I was spending too much money on services I wouldn't ever use so I started to look for a stable that had a more individual price plan for boarding. The stable was nice and the care was great but financially it wasn't a good fit anymore and I could spend my money more productively on other fun things like saddles, tack and, oh yes, my husband!

Julie

Chapter 9

Veterinarians, Farriers and
Other Professionals

Your horse is going to need a Veterinarian and a Farrier. It is important to find out what the barn offers and allows because if you are not thrilled with the "house veterinarian or farrier" that the stable uses, you might not have another option. It doesn't happen often, but once in a while you will hear of a stable not allowing another vet or farrier to come to their barn because they want to give all the business to their choice of vet and farrier. That kind of control for a stable may not be a good fit for you. Remember that if you move your horse to a stable that is run like this and you don't like the farrier they use, you might become displeased and frustrated by the limitations for "choices of care" that are imposed on the boarders. Make sure you read through these important questions in this chapter and then you can start to see how boarding stables and other equine professionals work together and how it will affect you. Ask the right questions so you don't have regrets later.

132. Can I choose my own veterinarian?

Most boarding stables will allow you to choose your own veterinarian, but when you are on a tour take the time to clarify their rules. I have heard of barns where there is a "house" veterinarian that took care of all the horses and using a different vet clinic was frowned upon. Just remember it is your horse and you should be able to choose which veterinarian you want for the medical needs of your horse. You also need to understand that there are specialty veterinarians who are skilled and very knowledgeable about certain issues in horses. Some vets might specialize in lameness while others specialize in teeth or other parts of the body. It is no different than a specialty doctor that you would see for an issue you are having. It can be a red flag if a stable won't allow the owner to select a vet to come to their barn and provide care to their horse. It may not be common practice, but you do hear about this type of situation occasionally. Hopefully you can avoid this problem by asking the right questions before selecting a stable for your horse.

133. Will you hold my horse for a vet appointment? Is there a holding fee?

If you need to have the veterinarian out for a routine appointment or an emergency and you can't be present for the appointment you can usually rely on the barn manager or an employee to hold your horse for you. This service can have a "holding fee" attached to it as is common for many stables. Some barns will have this service included in the price of the monthly board rate and others will have this service listed as TBD or To Be Determined depending on the situation. It is always best to ask first how the stable offers this service and the fees involved.

134. Can I bring in an equine massage therapist or other equine specialist to work on my horse?

There are many equine specialists that treat many different parts of the equine body all to improve health: reduce pain in joints and muscles and relieve stress or anxiety in a horse. The different types of specialist in the equine industry is truly expanding and improving the horse industry in many ways. Some of these equine professionals will specialize in medical approaches while others will use methodologies that may include light therapy, essential oils and other evolving holistic practices. Care is not just limited to your local vet clinic anymore when looking to improve your horse's health, well-being and physical agility. Most boarding stables do not have a problem with a boarder bringing in someone who is "non-traditional" in the sense of veterinary care but it will be beneficial to discuss alternative care with the barn manager when you are touring a stable so that you both are on the same page.

135. Is there a holding fee for the farrier if I can't be there?

If you can't be on-site for your horse's farrier appointment you will want to ask if someone can hold your horse for you. Often a stable will have a holding fee for this service but there are boarding barns that do offer this service as part of the monthly board rate. If your horse is well-behaved and stands nicely while in cross-ties then the farrier might not need anyone to hold the horse.

Check with the barn manager about their policy and more importantly, you need to ask your farrier what his policy is for working on a horse with or without someone holding the horse. Usually if a horse is very well behaved then the farrier will be happy to work on the horse without someone standing right there the entire time. Every farrier has their own way of doing things and you will want to discuss this with them first.

136. Will you turn my horse back outside after the farrier is done with him?

Most boarding stables will have someone turn a horse back outside for the day after their farrier appointment if you can't be there. But just like in anything else regarding your horse, you need to ask first because you might be looking at a facility that will not have someone on staff midday to turn your horse back outside or they may charge a fee for this service. This is one more thing to think about as you start to tour facilities and develop and prioritize your list of needs and expectations. This list will help you learn how each stable in your area operates and whether they will be a good fit for you and your horse.

Spring and Fall Shots

137. What shots are mandatory for spring and fall?

This is one of the most important questions you will need to ask when looking for a boarding stable. You need to find out what each stable requires for yearly vaccines and you will be surprised after going to a few stables by how different the requirements are from one area to another and from state to state. If a stable doesn't require vaccines, you may find yourself questioning their commitment to quality care. When it comes to the health of your horse, one thing you need to really think about is the increased risk of exposure to disease by another horse that wasn't vaccinated. You might do everything in your power to make sure your horse is vaccinated and properly cared for but if a serious infection goes through the barn it could affect your horse in one way or another, even if they are vaccinated. You are going to want to find out exactly how a stable handles vaccines and what their emergency protocol is if there is an outbreak of a virus or infection of some sort. I would also consider talking to your veterinarian and asking them what their thoughts are on certain vaccines and what they recommend for your horse.

A well-run stable is going to have a vet recommended vaccine protocol in place for spring and fall shots and you should ask the barn manager what it is and how compliance is monitored and enforced. If it is unclear what the barn manager recommends, or she says that she lets the boarders decide on vaccines then you have a huge problem! If only some of the horses are being vaccinated at the stable, then you might want to look elsewhere for a boarding stable.

138. Can I opt out of certain shots?

You can ask a barn manager if you can opt out of certain shots and they will tell you if they will consider it. Some horses have a strong reaction to certain shots especially senior horses. This is where it is always best to talk to your veterinarian

113

regarding your horse and vaccines and then you can talk to the barn manager. Hopefully if you like the stable then you both can work out an arrangement for your horse in a special needs case when it comes to vaccines. Don't be disappointed if the barn manager requires every horse to have full vaccines no matter the age of the horse. They have to do what they feel is best for the entire barn and every horse on the property. Remember that the barn manager has to look at the big picture when it comes to how it will affect the horses.

139. Can I give my horse his vaccines myself?

There are many vaccines you can purchase "over the counter" and if you normally give your horse his shots then you will want to make sure that it is okay to do. Many boarding stables will allow the boarder to vaccinate their own horse as long as they have proof that the vaccines were given.

140. What if my horse has a reaction to the shots or a specific shot? Will you give medication if my horse needs it?

Sometimes a horse will have a strong reaction to a shot and need some medication during the next day or two to counteract the reaction. If you are not able to administer the meds, then you will want to ask if the barn manager is able to offer this service. You will also want to find out if there is a fee for this service.

141. What do you require for vaccines or paperwork before I bring my horse to your barn?

Each boarding stable will have their own requirements for what is needed before the horse steps off of the trailer and into their new barn home. Often they will ask for proof of vaccinations and they will ask for a current Coggins for the horse. The Coggins test checks for Equine Infectious Anemia (EIA) antibodies in the horse's blood. Blood samples must be sent to a state approved laboratory. This test is often needed to take your horse to horse shows or horse stables and whenever you transport your horse across state lines. At each stable that you evaluate you should ask the barn owner what tests and paperwork they require before accepting a horse into their facility.

Deworming Protocol

142. What deworming program do you have for the barn?

This is another very important topic that you are going to want a clear answer on. Too many people view deworming horses as not important and at a boarding stable, with horses coming and going, it should be of the highest importance! Ask about their deworming program and if you don't understand it completely then I would talk to your veterinarian to find out what they recommend. The deworming program should be clear when explained and, more importantly, it should be rigorously enforced by the stable. This means that when it is time to deworm the horses, then *ALL* horses need to be dewormed according to best practice deworming protocols recommended during that timeframe.

The truth is most stables have a deworming program but, sadly, some do not enforce it and there may be horses that do not get dewormed for years! Protect your horse by choosing a stable that is diligent in making sure all horses are dewormed at the scheduled times of the year and the deworming schedule complies with the most recent veterinary protocols.

143. Can I use whatever dewormer I choose?

Normally a stable will have a deworming protocol that they follow that is recommended by equine veterinarians. It is important to rotate dewormers and they will usually send out a notice of what type of dewormer is recommend at a certain time of year. If the stable you are looking at doesn't send out a notice then you will want to check with your veterinarian on which dewormer you should use.

144. Can I deworm my horse myself or do you give it?

Some stables will deworm all the horses while others will have the horse owners do it themselves. Some boarding stables will not allow the boarders to deworm their horse (even if they want to) and they will administer the dewormer and keep track of the deworming records. Usually a stable will rotate dewormers and they will decide what will be given depending on the time of year. If your horse has had known issues with a certain type of dewormer then you need to discuss this with the barn manager and make sure you both agree on what you would like your horse to have.

145. Can you buy and administer the dewormer for my horse and is there a fee?

If you don't want to buy the dewormer or administer it then you can ask the barn manager if they will offer this service and what the fee is. Some stables will include dewormer and administration as part of the monthly board fee and then you never have to worry about it. Others will purchase and administer it upon request and then add it on to your board invoice at the end of the month.

146. Can you teach me how to deworm my horse?

Often a new horse owner will not know how to administer dewormer but want to learn how to do it correctly. Ask the barn manager if someone can teach you how to administer dewormer to your horse so that that you can do it in the future on your own.

147. Instead of the traditional dewormers on the market, can I use a more natural product for my horse?

There are many different types of dewormers and now there are more "natural" products for getting rid of worms. BUT BEWARE - not all these natural dewormers work as well as they advertise. If you ask a barn manager and they are willing to let you give your horse a natural dewormer then they may require a fecal count on your horse to see if the dewormer is working or if the shedding count has gone up.

You need to understand that a boarding stable has horses coming and going for all different reasons and it is much easier for a horse to become infested with worms at a boarding stable than in your own private homestead. Natural deworming doesn't always work optimally at a boarding stable because of all the exposures that can happen with horses coming in and leaving. The risks increase and that is why the traditional dewormers are a better choice for a boarding stable.

I had a situation at a boarding stable where the barn manager didn't require yearly shots or deworming! I was a new horse owner and never gave it a thought to ask about vaccines or deworming and the place was very clean and organized and I just assumed there wasn't a problem. After I was there for a while I started to notice the high turnover of horses coming and going and when I asked other boarders they told me that it was normal.

One day the vet was out to treat a horse who had been at the barn for years and the horse had been acting colicky, and on top of it, they had noticed a bunch of worms in his manure in his stall. This horse had worms and it turned out the horse hadn't been dewormed in years, which came as a total shock to me.

I started to panic about my horse so I made a veterinarian appointment to find out what I could do to prevent this happening with my horse. They did a fecal count but advised me that the barn manager needed to change their policy on deworming and make protocols more consistent in order to get the worm situation under control

A group of boarders got together and decided to talk with the barn manager about creating a system where all the horses are dewormed on time during each vet recommended period. The barn manager was open to this change and I thought everything was on track to get the worms under control but, unfortunately, there was no follow through by the barn manager and everything went back to the way it was.

In the end I had to move my horse because I couldn't keep him at a stable where I worried about his health and their vaccine and deworming program (or should I say lack of it!) was a huge part of it for me. I was sad to move and leave friends but I had to put my horse first.

Patricia

Chapter 10

Clinics and Other Activities

Are you looking for a stable that offers clinics or other activities? This will be an individual decision but if you want to be at an active barn then you need to ask the right questions. The size of a boarding stable does not reflect if they have clinics or activities. Many smaller stables will offer many clinics and activities on a smaller scale and that may be perfect for what you are looking for.

148. What types of clinics do you offer?

Clinics can be a huge benefit for a boarding stable. The stable does not need to be large to host clinics and the clinics can be focused on many different interests or disciplines. If you are a person that loves to continue learning and you do not have a trailer to travel off site, then you might want to ask if the stable you are considering offers clinics. Ask if they are open to a variety of clinics and how often they have them. If a stable has not had many clinics or any at all, then ask if you can help set one up. You might be able to get the ball rolling and suggest a certain clinician or specific subject that might interest the boarders at the barn.

149. Do you offer organized trail rides?

Many people love to trail ride and they want to ride with other people. If this is of interest to you then ask how often people trail ride at the stable and if they get together often on organized trail rides. Again, this is a situation where you might be the person to get these types of fun events started.

150. Where can we ride on the property?

As you tour a boarding stable you will want to know how much property the stable is on and where can you ride outside. Ask to walk some of the property and have the barn manager show you the outdoor amenities. If you like to ride outside then it is important to see what they have to offer for trails, open fields and outdoor riding arenas.

151. What other activities do you have at the barn?

A huge part of a boarding stable is the relationships between the boarders. Often an active barn will have activities on site or off site. These activities could be organized by the stable and they may even be organized by a group of boarders. If you are looking for a barn that does a lot of activities with a horse or without, then ask around and find a stable that has a reputation for doing lots of different fun things.

My first boarding experience was a hum-dinger to say the least. My parents had bought me my first horse and we chose a stable that was very close to my home so that I could ride my bike there after school and during the summer months. I wasn't old enough to drive a car yet but it was easy enough to ride my bike to the stable. I had been there a couple of months and I thought everything seemed fine until one day I went to see my horse and my horse was gone! I found out from another boarder that the trainer had taken my horse on a trail ride with other people and wouldn't be back until later that day. This was long before cell phones (the 1980's!) and there was no way to contact this trainer so I had to wait all day.

I went home and told my dad and together we went back to the stable to talk with the trainer who also was also the owner of the stable. The trainer explained that she had told us (when we first moved my horse there) that she would be doing this once in a while as part of her lesson program and it was good for my horse. My father couldn't remember the trainer saying this and he didn't like the fact that she took our horse without even contacting us first. We decided to look for a different boarding stable.

Many years later, I still remember that first boarding experience and I still think about it when looking at stables as an adult in my fifties. You never forget those traumatic experiences and that one was a big one for a little girl.

Tamera

Chapter 11

Is The Stable a Good Fit For You?

Finding a stable that is a good fit will not only revolve around your horse but it needs to be a good fit for you too, especially if you are going to be out at the stable often. You need to feel completely comfortable at the stable and also feel like you can ask for help if something comes up. The atmosphere should be positive whether you are looking at a small boarding stable or a larger one with a lot of activity. There should be a sense of organization, professionalism and cooperation. Look for boarders who support one another without judgement. Look for a stable with a "No Drama Allowed" atmosphere! You need to really think about the needs you have personally and then you can better find a stable that meets your needs and expectations.

152. Can my child ride alone and unsupervised? What is the age when he can ride without an adult near?

When looking for a stable where your child can ride make sure to find out the age requirements for riding without adult supervision and any other rules about children's activities at the stable. This is completely up to the barn owner's discretion and much it of will depend on the maturity and horsemanship level of the child and the type of horse they will be riding. "Green on green" which means a beginner rider and young barely broke/trained horse is not a good combination to leave alone, especially when the rider/handler is a child. An older "been there/done that" calm horse or pony is often a much better match for a green rider, but it still needs to be approved by the barn owner.

A child who has riding skills and experience and shows signs of maturity when handling their horse and has a calm and quiet horse will often be approved to ride alone long before an older child with a horse way beyond their skill level. It is an individual decision and so much needs to be looked at before the barn manager will make a final decision. It is all about safety and not taking unnecessary risks.

153. Are there kids at the barn?

If you are looking for a barn with kids for your child to ride with then you are going to want to ask if the stable has many children who ride. Some stables will have lots of kids and lessons going on all the time while other barns might be geared towards older people. Asking a few simple questions will help you decide if a certain stable is right for you and your child.

154. I am looking for a barn with older people – Are there many older people who like to trial ride?

Often a person will buy a horse for the first time after they have retired or raised their own family. Some older people prefer a stable where there are no kids riding and then other older people absolutely love to have kids around. You just need to find out what you want and what you feel comfortable with. A lot will depend on how the stable is run. A well-run boarding stable with barn rules that are followed and enforced by even the young people will make it pleasant for everyone.

155. What kind of turnover do you have with clients leaving and new ones coming in?

Turnover at a boarding stable is hard on everyone including the boarders. Everyone likes a business that is consistent day in and day out, especially if you

125

are dealing with animals of any kind. This is equally important for the people who are at the barn every day. There are many reasons why a stable could have high turnover and it is something that warrants conversation and understanding. What can make this situation even sadder is that often you will become friends with other people at the barn and then one day you find out that one of your riding partners is leaving due to issues at the barn. This can make it a stressful time for you as you decide what you are going to do. The barn becomes a very social place where people become friends and like to ride and hang out and talk about their horses and life. A lot of change and turnover in a boarding stable disrupts this routine and socialization and can be upsetting for the clients who board there. A stable truly does become a barn family with strong bonds. It is important to realize that boarders' requirements and interests can change and horses will get moved for various reasons. Often is has nothing to do with the care a stable provides for the horses.

156. Does someone live on the property?

This is an important question to ask because you will want to make sure someone is around if there is an accident of any kind either with a horse or person. Most stables have someone living on the property but a rare few will not have anyone in permanent residence. It will be a personal choice or preference for you, and it is simply a matter of what you feel comfortable with.

157. Do you have any openings or is there a waiting list?

You will want to ask if there are any openings and, if not, how soon does the barn manager expect to have openings? A stable that is well-run will have a great reputation and will most likely have a waiting list for people who would like to bring their horse to the stable. If a stable has a waiting list and you like the facility, then **get on it!** Don't be discouraged because a barn has a waiting list. A barn owner usually doesn't have an idea of when someone is going to leave and if a client of multiple horses gives their thirty-day notice then that will open a few stalls at the same time. A waiting list is usually only good for so many months and then many of those people who were on it have moved their horse to a different stable and have settled in. At that point they do not want to move their horse again. Moving a horse is a BIG deal and it can be equally stressful on the horse and the owner of the horse. If you like a stable then get on their waiting list and, hopefully, something will open soon for you

I was looking for a stable with kids so that my daughter could ride with other people and show with them on the weekends. The first stable I toured looked like a wonderful place and it felt like it would be a good fit for my daughter. I never gave any thought to the daily care of the horses since my first priority was a positive environment for my daughter.

We moved our horse there and my daughter started taking lessons with an on-site trainer. After a month I started to notice that my daughter's horse who is normally very quiet and steady became very nervous and uptight. He also started to lose weight.

I talked with the barn manager and told her my concerns and she said that she didn't notice anything. I started to ask the other boarders if they noticed anything out in the herds because we were not able to get out during the day due to school and work. One of the boarder's told me that they noticed that our horse always stood by himself and when the horses were eating he paced the fence a lot. They said that he would eat but it was after many of the other horses were full and were not as interested in food.

I talked to the barn manager about what I was told and asked her if she had noticed anything. She told me that my horse was doing absolutely wonderful and she didn't see him pacing at all.

I knew my horse very well and I knew something wasn't right so I decided to drive by early in the morning after the horses were fed and watch from the barn. Sure enough my horse couldn't get to the hay and was being chased off of the round bale. He looked stressed and was pacing and I felt horrible! I went to the barn manager and had her come look and it didn't seem to bother her at all. I explained that his personality had changed and he was losing weight, but she still didn't seem to care. I finally asked her if I could move my horse to a different herd and she said she had no other options. I realized at that moment that this was a bad situation at the stable and I needed to move my horse as soon as possible. My easy going boy was not doing well at this stable.

We moved by the end of the week to a new stable and my horse became his old self very fast and my daughter was back to riding her calm and steady guy. I learned so much from that situation and now I know a little more about what to look for when it comes to boarding stables.

Lynne

Chapter 12

Red flags To Look For in
a Boarding Stable

I felt it was important to create a list of "Red flags" that you should be aware of when touring a stable or already boarding at one. These are things that you often wouldn't notice unless you ask for references or talk to other people. It may be something that the barn manager will not admit to if there was a problem – after all, they want you as a client. Be smart and do a little investigating so you don't have heartache later if you find out you need to move your horse because of unseen issues at your stable.

- **High turnover** – If a boarding stable has a high turnover of clients then you will want to find out why. It is perfectly fine to ask the barn manager what kind of turnover they have with clients and horses. Turnover creates instability in the herds and that can lead to many other problems and accidents or injuries become higher as new horses come into the herds. Remember what we talked about earlier, that every time a new horse comes into a herd, they need to figure out the pecking order of the herd all over again.

  If you are hearing that a stable has high turnover because of the daily care, then that is a red flag. Find out what they mean by daily care. Are they running out of hay? Are they running out of bedding? Are they not following through on what they advertise they offer for quality care or amenities? Is the barn making unexpected changes that many of the boarders are not happy with? Do they raise the board rates often or in extremely large increments? Are the horses spending long periods of time without water? Are the horses getting hurt frequently due to poor herd management? Are horses getting sick frequently? The more you investigate when you hear someone say that a barn has high turnover, the more you will be able to decipher what is going on and then you can make a knowledgeable decision on what you want to do next.

A barn owner will never be able to please all his clients and you will have people come and go no matter how good the barn takes care of the horses. Some people are just not happy no matter where they are. But if the turnover becomes very frequent and the word on the street is that it's about the lack of care, then that is important to take note of. Don't compromise the horse's care because you like the stable.

- **Drama** – The fastest way to ruin a boarding stable is drama! If you are looking at a stable and you hear rumors that there is a lot of drama, then I would look closer. Remember the adage that one rotten apple can ruin the bushel…the same is true in boarding stables as one person who thrives on creating drama can be disruptive to the calm environment of a stable resulting in management mediation and potential expulsion. **A barn that has drama means that it is lacking leadership from the barn owner and barn manager and that is a red flag.** Just remember that a well-run stable has strong leadership and little to no drama.

- **Rules are not followed** – If a barn has rules but they are not enforced then you are going to have problems and at a larger facility you will have chaos! Find out if the rules are enforced and enforced equally among all clients.

- **Money issues** – It will be hard to know if a boarding stable is having money issues but there are some signs. If things do not get fixed after they are broken then that could be a sign that they don't have the money to fix them. It doesn't always mean the stable has money issues but it is something to watch especially if the stable starts to go downhill. If the barn owner starts asking its clients if they will pay ahead and "get a discount" it could be a sign of money issues.

I heard a story of a boarding stable that had asked its boarders if they would pay their board for three months in advance and they would give them a discount. Most of the boarders paid in advance because they were happy to get the discount and everything seemed great. A month later the stable left a note to its boarders that it was closing its doors in thirty days! They also hadn't purchased enough hay and were running out. The stable fell apart overnight and I am not sure if any of the boarders got their money back for the extra months they had paid. I am not trying to scare you, and this may sound extreme but in business the craziest things can happen. It is just something to be aware of when a stable begins making sudden deals with its boarders.

- **No consistency** - If you hear that a stable is lacking consistency in its feeding schedule or daily chore program then take a closer for other issues. If you are told one thing one day and then it changes the next and this becomes a common thing at your stable, then that is a red flag that the stable is lacking consistency. A business without consistency will have problems. Just be mindful of that.

- **Messy barn** – If you drive up to a stable and look around and see junk everywhere even out in the paddocks and pastures then that is a huge red flag about how the place is run and how that will impact your horse in regards to his safety. Horses can get hurt on anything in a heartbeat. A messy boarding stable is a red flag that things are not organized, and safety may not be a priority.

- **Safety hazards** – As you take a tour, look over everything for possible safety hazards. Are the stalls in good condition? Are they missing boards on the stall walls that a horse could get their leg stuck through? Are there nails protruding in places? Do you see unsafe practices with riders and their horses that could lead to someone getting hurt? Do you see fences that are not mended? Start to make yourself aware of safety hazards so that you don't get a call that your horse was hurt and the vet is on their way.

The truth is everyone's idea of red flags and safety hazards will differ a bit depending on what they feel comfortable with. You need to decide what is best for you and your horse and not rely on how others feel. Don't compromise the care and safety of you or your horse even if others don't think it's a big deal.

I have had some "red flag" experiences in boarding stables and those are the times that I wish I would have followed my gut feelings first.

I was at a barn where everyone seemed nice when we first arrived, but I could quickly feel this negative atmosphere at the barn. I started to experience what "barn drama" is all about first-hand and it was awful. People were talking about each other and stirring up drama and really making it uncomfortable for others to ride and enjoy themselves at the barn.

There was also this underlying feeling that one particular boarder was running the show and had preferential treatment over the other boarders. This person seemed to have "better" tack spots for her saddles and tack and more space than the rest of the people who boarded there. She also was able to do things that went against the barn rules without any consequences and that started to upset other riders especially when it came to following barn hours. This person seemed to be able to do whatever she wanted while others could not.

The barn manager was young and, I would guess, somewhat inexperienced when dealing with clients and issues so it was probably easier to let this boarder do what she wanted. After all, confrontation is always hard. In the end, I decided it was time to look for a new stable that had a positive atmosphere and where everyone was treated equally in all situations.

The best thing I could do for my mental well-being was to move to a new stable that was encouraging and supportive of all its clients and everyone was treated equal. Beware of a barn with drama!!

Rachel

Chapter 13

Common Mistakes When Choosing a Horse Boarding Stable

If you have moved your horse to a boarding stable and start to seriously regret it six months later, you are not alone by any stretch of the imagination. In fact, I would dare say that almost every person who has ever owned a horse has at least one boarding story of regret. BUT with each poor decision comes a lot of learning and that is a great thing! This chapter is about some of the common mistakes that most horse owners make only because they didn't know better and had to learn the hard way. Remember the goal of the book is to educate you and save you from heartache, if possible, and that comes from gaining knowledge and then using discernment when looking for a barn you can call home for your horse and you.

I have included some of the most common mistakes that have been made (I have made them too when I was a boarder myself) and you are not alone. You are in good company! Now let's learn so you can improve your horse's life starting today.

Cheaper isn't always better - You get what you pay for

Truth – Owning a horse is expensive - plain and simple so being sensible with your money is smart. Learning what a stable offers for amenities and care is very important so you need to shop around and look at stables in your price range. I have learned over the years that people will choose a boarding stable (a cheaper one) based solely on price but without doing their homework to see how good the care is or how well maintained the stable is. They have not done their homework to find out how knowledgeable the staff is in horse care or herd management. They choose a stable because it is cheaper and it ends up costing them a lot more down the road. Their horse may lose weight or become stressed. He could get hurt due to preventable safety hazards that are everywhere and not corrected. You could end up with large vet bills because you are were trying to save money.

I get it, we all want to save money and horses are not cheap to own. But if you are going to care for this huge animal that you love then may I suggest looking for other ways to save money so you can afford to keep your horse at a stable where the care is top notch and you won't be worrying constantly.

If you are new to horse ownership and boarding then this may seem a little dramatic but it's not at all! I was a boarder for many years when I was young so I know what it is like to worry about your horse and not have any control. As a barn owner of a large boarding stable, I hear stories all the time from new clients who were at a previous place where things went downhill fast and they were in constant worry about their horse.

There are a lot of good boarding stables out there and the barns that are run professionally and consistently are going to demand a higher monthly board rate. It cost a lot of money to keep a stable running and in excellent condition and the ongoing repairs, maintenance and supplies cost more than most boarders would imagine.

You get what you pay for most of the time, so I encourage you to do your homework and educate yourself the best that you can on horse care and then start evaluating boarding stables by using your requirement checklist for every stable you are considering. Once you understand your priorities you will be in a better position to make an objective decision on what is best for your horse and you. You may pay a little more for a high-quality boarding stable, but you will never regret it once you experience the value and importance of top-notch care.

More expensive – It must be better

You might assume that the boarding stables that are the most expensive in your area must have the best care but that is not always the case. This is where this book will really help you. You have read all the questions and answers and now you are starting to get a real feel for what good care is for *your* horse and what *you* want in a stable. Use that knowledge.

The monthly board rate that is set for a boarding facility will depend greatly on many factors that are behind the scenes. You won't know what the owner's monthly business mortgage is or how much they paid for hay and bedding unless they tell you. You won't know how much fuel they use or how much the electric bill is monthly. Boarding stables typically have business mortgages, multiple insurance coverages including Care, Custody and Control insurance (which is for the horses on the property in the stable's care) and that is just the beginning. Property taxes and workers compensation is also absorbed into the board rates. The expenses and expenditures add up very fast. It is important to look at the amenities a stable provides but understand that every amenity a stable has to offer will need to be maintained and it all takes labor and money. Some of the hidden fees and costs to run the stable will never be made known to the clients. If a boarding stable is set up correctly, then all the costs to keep it running year-round should determine the monthly board rates.

What matters most is the care of the horses! You could decide to board your horse at the most expensive place in your area but if the care is lacking and your horse is starting to become stressed then you have a big problem. If the communication is poor between the barn manager and clients, then you need to be concerned. THAT IS WHY THE QUESTIONS IN THIS BOOK ARE SO IMPORTANT. There are no guarantees that a more expensive stable will automatically be better. You need to be smart when evaluating stables and I encourage you to look at many stables before making any decisions. Shop around because you are going to learn so much from each stable and your knowledge about how facilities operate is going to grow exponentially just by touring each of them. Take your time and do this part right and you won't regret it later.

Bling, bells and whistles

We have certainly become people who like bells and whistles. Many people love the newer cars because they practically do everything for us and have many bells and whistles to make our driving experience better. That may be great for driving a car but when it comes to your horse; I encourage you to keep things simple. When looking for a stable, don't get sucked in by all the bells and whistles a barn may offer. Look deeper into the daily care of the horses. Consider how the horses look: do they look healthy and content or do they look stressed or even underweight for many of them?

A barn that has bling, bells and whistles may look inviting and may offer lots of perks. They may have a cappuccino machine in their lounge or a television with cable for people to watch a show while their child rides their horse in a lesson. They may offer cameras where you can watch your horse from home 24/7! They may have European stalls with fancy chandelier lighting hanging from the ceiling. You may think I am joking but I am not! I have been in stables that were much fancier than most homes and, yes, I have been in a barn with a chandelier hanging from the ceiling. STOP! It doesn't mean the care of the horse is good. Don't get caught up in the bling, do your homework and make sure the care is top notch. If it turns out - that the fancy stable that you are drooling over also gives phenomenal care, then go for it and enjoy the added perks of a hot cappuccino under chandler lighting while watching your favorite Netflix show!   I couldn't help myself; I had to put a little humor in this book!

<u>Picturesque</u>

Your first impression of a boarding stable will start to form just as you are driving up the driveway. You will look around and your eyes will be trying to take it all in as fast as possible. It might be summertime and the horses are all out on pasture and it looks like a Kentucky horse farm you would see in a magazine or book. It might have this "old fashioned" look from the barns of yesterday that give you a feeling of comfort and even nostalgia from a time long gone. It could be a state-of-the-art, brand new barn and it makes your heart skip a beat!

Each one of us has a picture in our mind of what the perfect barn will look like and it is different for all of us. Yes, it is important for the stable to look clean and orderly, but you need to look deeper when touring a barn. You still need to make sure it is the correct fit for your horse. Be smart and ask the right questions to make sure the stable is what you are looking for.

You also need to realize that a boarding stable will take on a different feel and look with each season. It would be safe to say that most boarding stables look fantastic during the summertime when the grass is green and the sun is shining. But if you live in a place where you have all four seasons, then springtime after a long hard winter can be UGLY! The place will look brown for a couple of months until the grasses grow and green up. The paddocks will be muddy from the frost coming out of the ground and the springtime rains make it worse. The picture you viewed last summer has faded away for the time being and that is normal for any farm. Don't be disappointed but understand that it is all a part of enduring seasonal farm life, caring for animals and tolerating the influence of "mother nature". Before you know it, summer will be here again. At the end of the day it is all about the care and that will always be the most important element in horse boarding.

The barn manager was so sweet during the tour!

When you take a tour of a boarding stable it is important to get a good feel for the barn manager and how they run the stable. After all, most of your communication will be with them. It is easy to get lost in the fact that the barn manager may have been the sweetest person and you instantly felt comfortable around her, but you need to know more. How is she as a leader when she is running the barn? How is she with her employees? What is her horse knowledge and how does she handle emergencies? Is she organized when it comes to how the daily chores are done? It is important to find out how she will communicate with you when a problem situation arises. You are going to want to ask other current boarders how the barn manger runs the stable.

Don't compromise the care of your horse for location

We would all love to be close to our horse especially, if we work and are on a limited time schedule, BUT don't choose a stable just because it is a convenient location. If you do your homework (reading this book and learning as much as you can about good horse care) and learn exactly what is best for your horse and you, and coincidentally the ideal stable is just down the street - then that is a bonus! But if you find out that the stable that is the best fit for your horse and the care is top notch is ten miles away, then drive the distance and you will never regret it. THERE IS NOTHING WORSE THAN WORRYING ABOUT YOUR HORSE AND THE CARE HE IS RECEIVING WHEN YOU ARE NOT THERE. Don't compromise the care of your horse for location.

As a boarder I paid for stall board where my horse would be brought in every night and outside during the day. I was told that the horses would be turned out by 7am and in by 6 pm.

Numerous times I would come out to the barn and it would be 10 or 11 in the morning and my horse would still be inside and he had not been fed morning grain yet. In the evenings I would come out and my horse would be outside past 8pm. My horse was also on a special diet and I would bag up his grain in gallon size zip lock bags for easy feeding, labeled AM and PM. I found out that the owner of the facility was feeding one of her own horses my grain. I knew coming into the barn that my gut told me it wasn't as "perfect" as it seemed from the outside and I should have trusted my gut.

I was not a "new to the horse world" owner at this time ... and I thought that I did my homework. Even after I had seen "red flags" of some lack of care in the facility (poor fencing, not kept clean, unorganized) and even word of mouth from past boarders, I still chose to move my horse there. I thought that my bagging of the grain to keep track of it and have it easily fed and paying the extra to have my horse in every night would limit the concerns that I had coming in as a boarder there. But at the end of the day I had made a poor choice.

I ended up moving my horse to the facility because it was closer to my home. The stable I came from provided excellent care but was an hour drive from home which is why I put my blinders on as a horse owner and wanted to have my horse closer to home. I learned a lot from that experience and now I am happy to drive farther to make sure my horse is getting the best care.

Anne

Chapter 14

When a Boarding Stable Works

I felt compelled to write one last quick chapter that talks about the things that make a boarding stable wonderful. The first thing I need to say is THERE IS NO PERFECT BOARDING STABLE. Most barn owners and managers will try their best to create healthy living conditions for the horses in their care, but every person will have a different view of what that is. That is why it is so important for you to find the right fit for you. But if you do your homework and continually learn about your horse and what you want in a boarding stable then you will find the place that best meets your needs and expectations. Remember that you will likely need to compromise on some things that you want in a boarding stable, but you will now be able to evaluate when to compromise and when to move on to another facility.

It is important to remember that, like any other business, a boarding stable will change and evolve as the business grows. There is a huge learning curve with new boarding stables as the barn owner and manager try to define exactly what they want for their stable. It happened with my stable and through it all I continued to learn and provide better service for my clients – but most of it involved some change and adjustments for everyone. Barn owners and managers need to learn what works best at their stables regarding daily chores, herd management and client relations. It takes time, but when a stable finds the sweet spot in daily operations, chores, communication and client relations, it starts operating like a fine oiled machine. That is a great sign that the boarding stable is working well.

Signs that a boarding stable works well

When a boarding stable works for both you and your horse you will find that you can relax and let go of your concerns, knowing that your horse is consistently well cared for and observed for any signs of stress, injury or illness. You won't have to worry about the care of your horse so you can confidently go on vacation and enjoy yourself! When a boarding stable works, you won't have to guess what is going on at the barn. Good communication will be a priority and equally important for the barn manger and his clients. When a boarding stable works, you will find yourself in a positive and encouraging atmosphere where people are respectful and forgiving when mistakes are made. When a boarding stable works, you don't need to wonder what kind of mood the barn owner is in (even though they are human and have bad days just like you) when they walk in the barn or feel like you are on walking on eggshells. When a boarding stable works, you can ask questions in a safe, welcoming environment. When a boarding stable works, your horsemanship will start to grow because you are in a place where learning is easy and non-judgmental. When a boarding stable works, you will see it in your horse's behavior and over-all well-being. He will be content and so will you.

You are going to make lifelong friends at the barn and share more than just horses with many of them. You will experience the joy of watching someone learn something new with their horse and they will share in your accomplishments as well. You will laugh with each other often and cry with each other at times and you will become a barn family. You will grow in your horsemanship skills in ways you never imagined, and you will find yourself one day helping someone else who is a new horse owner and needs some encouragement and guidance as they navigate horse ownership and boarding stables. That is when a boarding stable works well!

Don't underestimate the impact that a stable can have on the lives of the people in it.

I was introduced to the barn at a time when my life was consumed by anxiety and depression caused by a high-stress job and family. After sharing my struggles with a horse-owning colleague, she suggested that taking riding lessons might be good therapy.

I entered my barn as a student of the resident trainer. It wasn't long before I had a half-lease on a lesson horse and was out there three days a week. I became friends with the trainer and her entourage. Even though I was only a student, the owners were friendly and expressed appreciation for how I respected the place and followed the rules. The barn quickly became the place which released me from all of the anxiety and stress of life.

Some months later, the trainer announced her plans to go elsewhere, taking most of my friends and my lesson horse with her. I was devastated. I had a choice: leave the barn with my trainer, horse and friends, or, stay at the barn, find a new teacher, my own horse and make friends with boarders who were staying. I spent a lot of time in tears wondering what to do.

While this was going on, the barn owners were always kind and friendly. They told me that they would be happy if I stayed and would be inviting in new teachers and trainers. The boarders started telling me about the high standard of care at this barn, how the owners watched over the herd and how secure they felt about the health and safety of their horses. The choice was clear: I could find a new trainer, horse and friends — but there is no other barn like this one.

I stayed because the owners made this barn the best it could be for the people and the horses. I have never regretted the choice.

Jane

About the Author

Sheri lives in Neenah, Wisconsin. She has two daughters and she owns and operates Vinland Stables alongside her husband David. Sheri has been both a boarder and now a barn owner and has truly experienced life on both sides of the fence. For the last fifteen years, Sheri has had the privilege of taking care of other people's horses at her barn. After years of running a boarding facility she now does consulting for barn owners and managers that are working to improve their boarding operation. Besides writing books, she is also a blogger and a speaker who enjoys talking with other professionals in all areas of the horse industry. In her free time she loves hanging out with her family and watching movies or getting together with friends. Life is pretty simple these days and she wouldn't have it any other way.

Sheri's Books and Website

You can catch Sheri's blog articles every week at

www.probarnmanagement.com

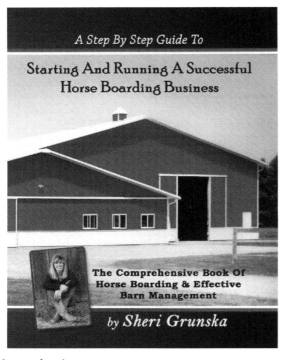

A Step By Step Guide To Starting and Running A Successful Horse Boarding Business.

The comprehensive book of horse boarding & effective barn management.

This book is being recognized and used in College Equine Programs across the country and is a fantastic resource for starting and running a horse business.

You can find all of Sheri's books on Amazon.com

What It Really Takes To Start and Run
A Horse Business
And how to do it right the first time

This is Sheri and David's story of starting their horse boarding stable which came with many mistakes and triumphs along way. It is a bold honest look into business ownership in the equine industry and how to avoid some of the pitfalls that can come with it.

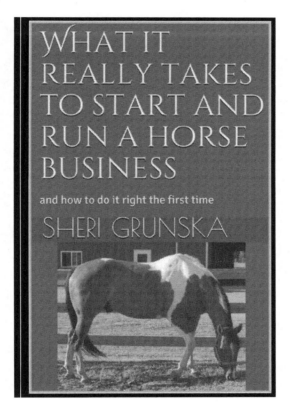

You can find this book on Amazon.com

One Horsewoman to Another
Trading in Your High Heels for Muddy Work Boots and Finding Courage, Confidence and Joy in ALL Of It!

From corporate chic to horse stable disaster, this book is perfect for any woman working with horses in any arena of the equine industry. It will delight you in every way and you will start to grow and become the businesswoman you are deep inside.

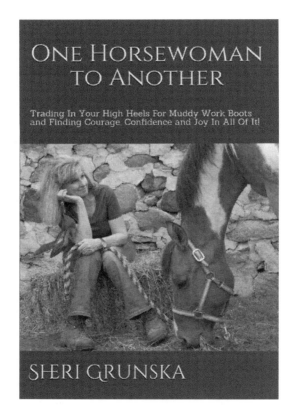

You can find this book on Amazon.com

Caring For Horses With a Servant's Heart – A daily devotional for the equine professional and the horse lover in all of us.

This book is 365 horse stories that will inspire and encourage you every day of the year! This book will take your through all four seasons and life on a horse farm and it is a bold and honest devotional that will tug at your heart strings and make you laugh out loud. The perfect book to start out your day.

You can find this book on Amazon.com

Quarter Horse mare ① education in Equine Behavior
10 years old   ② Barn management
Calm   ③ set up for emergenc[?]
Hard turnout   Power outages - earthquake - Fi[?]
Stall night/grains/suppliments
2nd command current mare herd (6)

Trails off property
Trailer parking
Large indoor arena - good footing - training
indoor bath room   items
   Rt Barn / clicker / western training poles
What type of riders?
How busy is the barn - Arena busy times -?
Higher level of attentiveness - well being of horse mental/ph[?]
Sound principles of care.
Business relationship - with owner
Boarding stables - w/o trainer excusive
Hot/Cold wash stall to rinse wash horse
Turnout 8~5
Stall 10x12 ↑
Footing for stalls - Bedding - How often cleaned?
   Refresh bedding daily
Salt/mineral Blocks
FANS - WArm wEAther / heater H2o Buckets winte[?]
   extra charge for electricity
Access to clean fresh H2o + in stall how often ar[?]
WAter buckets cleaned?   154 any soap used?
Are automatic H2o checked daily? How often are
those cleaned?

ovgn Board - Questions 35 →

Made in the USA
Coppell, TX
30 October 2021